COLLABORATIVE ADVANTAGE

COLLABORATIVE ADVANTAGE

How Organizations Win by Working Together

Elizabeth Lank

First published 2006 by
PALGRAVE MACMILLAN
Houndmills, Basingstoke, Hampshire RG21 6XS and
175 Fifth Avenue, New York, N.Y. 10010
Companies and representatives throughout the world

PALGRAVE MACMILLAN is the global academic imprint of the Palgrave
Macmillan division of St. Martin's Press, LLC and of Palgrave Macmillan Ltd.
Macmillan® is a registered trademark in the United States, United Kingdom and
other countries. Palgrave is a registered trademark in the European Union and
other countries.

ISBN-13: 978-1-4039-9345-8
ISBN-10: 1-4039-9345-9

This book is printed on paper suitable for recycling and made from fully
managed and sustained forest sources.

A catalogue record for this book is available from the British Library.

A catalog record for this book is available from the Library of Congress.

Editing and origination by
Curran Publishing Services, Norwich

10 9 8 7 6 5 4 3 2 1
15 14 13 12 11 10 09 08 07 06

Printed and bound in China

For Keith, Michael and Anna

Contents

Preface

On January 18, 2005, the heads of state of France, Germany, Great Britain, and Spain joined with several thousand guests for the unveiling in Toulouse of Airbus's latest aircraft, the Airbus 380. Unveiling the largest and most technologically advanced passenger aircraft in the world, a full-length double-decker capable of carrying more than 550 passengers, the ceremony was the culmination of many years of effort. This achievement was the result of collaboration and coordination between the major parts of Airbus in four different countries, and a raft of airline customers, parts suppliers, and other stakeholders such as the 60 major airports that contributed to the design process.

Airbus, a company with 52,000 employees around the world, has two major shareholders: the European Aeronautic Defence and Space Company (EADS), which owns 80 percent of the company, and British Aerospace, which owns 20 percent. EADS itself came into being in the year 2000 by combining three different organizations: French Aerospatiale Matra, CASA (Construcciones Aeronáuticas SA) of Spain, and the German Daimler Chrysler Aerospace AG (Dasa). So although Airbus is now one legal entity, it is in reality a confederation that is cross-organizational, transnational, and yet still able to deliver a hugely challenging product such as the A380. Airbus has demonstrated its ability to create collaborative advantage—and rather than viewing Airbus as unique, it is the premise of this book that it is just one of the pioneers of a way of working that will become the norm as the 21st century unfolds.

How many collaborative ventures is your organization connected with? I suspect the answer is more than you think. This is not just about formal membership of associations and industry bodies—it is about the day-to-day challenges of task forces, steering groups, project teams, research consortia, benchmarking clubs, and a whole range of small and large networks that underpin the knowledge-based economy in which we now live. This book is about the many and varied forms that cross-organizational collaboration takes, the imperatives that drive the creation of such relationships, and the practical steps that make the difference between a successful outcome and a potentially monumental waste of money and time. It is based on the premise that collaborative working is here to stay. With the constant pressures on resources and the ever-increasing expectations of stakeholders, going it alone is no longer an option. Yet even in this networked world, we still cling to a world view that the only organizational unit that matters, that should be monitored and measured, that develops competitive advantage (or not), is the single organizational unit: a firm, a government department, a charity. In fact every organization exists within in its own unique ecosystem of cross-organizational relationships, which either add or subtract value from the organization, depending on the skill with which it manages them.

The hypothesis that this book develops is as follows: succeeding as a single organizational entity is increasingly dependent on succeeding as a participant in different collaborative processes. Competitive advantage is now dependent on establishing collaborative advantage. Without the knowledge and skill to work with other organizations, it is likely that your organization will wither on the economic vine. But make no mistake about it: working effectively with different organizations takes great skill and determination.

In the chapters that follow, we shall explore what effective collaboration really entails. We start with a map of the territory, defining some key terms and looking at the main drivers that motivate organizations to engage in a collaborative process. We then consider the key activities that will require time and attention in order for any collaborative venture—of any size or scope—to succeed. Subsequent chapters explore not so much the why and the what, but the how—the different facets of getting value from collaborating with others, illustrated with stories from a kaleidoscope of different organizations from across the globe. This is not just about what works: there are direct warnings about some of the common pitfalls that await organizations that have not taken enough time to prepare—or invested enough effort to sustain—their collaborative efforts.

We also spend some time exploring the challenge of internal collaboration, as internal boundaries can sometimes feel as impermeable as external ones. Collaborative advantage can also be gained by joining up capabilities within one organization—and that becomes an excellent foundation for joining up with external partners.

Finally, we reflect on the strategic challenge of building up collaborative capacity. Beyond the why, what, and how of collaborative working, there is the question of who: that is to say, who within your organization has the capability to connect effectively with people from other organizations in order to deliver the desired results.

This book is intended for those who are either involved directly in cross-organizational collaboration, or expect to be in the future—and for those who already understand the strategic importance of this area and wish to improve the overall capability of their organization to collaborate effectively. It has been written in the hope that it will save you time, effort, and money, by enabling you to learn from the practical experience of others—and that it will strengthen your resolve to build your own organization's collaborative advantage.

Acknowledgments

It goes without saying that a book about collaboration cannot be the product of one person's experience. I am grateful to all of the busy people who found time to talk to me about their personal experience of working in collaborative ventures of many kinds, and who were happy to share the ups and downs that they went through, as well as the valuable lessons that they learnt. Thank you all.

I have also appreciated the ideas and support from family, friends, and colleagues who have challenged, encouraged, and helped me make connections that I might not otherwise have made. Particular thanks go to Mark Bernard, Chris Collison, Alison Donaldson, Peter Hewkin, Rob Inglis, Graeme Mackay, Irena Sobolewska, Patrick Spaven, Nicki Tanner, Egbert Veldman, Gill Warland and Jane Wonnacott. To my parents Alli and Connie Lank, thank you too for the several decades of encouragement that preceded this project. Thank you also to my research assistant Giordana Bongioanni who did a great job unearthing all sorts of interesting stories that might not otherwise have come to light.

My immediate family has coped admirably with the consequences of their wife and mother dedicating herself to "The Book" over many months—so Keith, Michael and Anna, this one's for you.

EAL

Introduction

No organization is an island

Today's information and communication technologies mean that major events in any part of the world are instant news throughout the globe, that it is as easy to shop at an online store on another continent as it is to drive to your nearest shopping mall, that you can admire the picture of a newborn baby on a family member's website or on your mobile phone just hours after the child is born. We are truly in a global village, and our lives today are set within a much greater web of connections than any previous generation would recognize. As individuals we are experiencing this connected world—and so, inevitably, are organizations.

People spend their working lives inside a fascinating mixture of different organizations, with enormous variation in size, scope, culture, aims, and approaches. These organizations have many different objectives—making money for shareholders, delivering products and services, serving citizens, raising money to help others. Yet whatever business they are in, all organizations face the universal experience of an ever-increasing pressure on resources and ever more demanding expectations of stakeholders, whoever they may be.

Much has been written over the years about different strategic choices available to organizational leaders, in order to make best use of the resources available to them and to meet or exceed the expectations of their stakeholders. Not entirely surprisingly, the unit of analysis has generally been one specific organization and the choices it makes about its own markets, competencies, and processes. However, it is self-evident that no single organization can be the best, the quickest, the most cost-effective at everything. Working with others to bring the right combination of skills, experience, and resources to the job at hand is becoming a necessity in a world that moves as quickly, and demands as much, as ours does today. Information and communication technology has dramatically lowered the transaction costs of collaborating—it is now much easier to find and connect with a whole range of organizational partners. It is increasingly clear that going it alone is no longer a viable option for any organization.

1

Organizational ecosystems

It is not that connections between organizations are a new phenomenon. Every organization connects, and has always connected, to its customers, suppliers, and partners in some way. However, the perspective on these relationships has generally been a transactional one: you sell to customers, you buy from suppliers, you negotiate partnerships. This book will develop a different perspective, taking the view that organizations can no longer be treated as independent entities, merely transacting with other organizations. The connections that organizations choose to make with other organizations are as much a strategic choice as the investments they make in product research, service enhancement, or skills development. Rather than simply viewing these relationships as by-products of other strategic decisions, we shall put them center stage. While accepting that transactional relationships still exist—that is, straightforward commercial relationships like buying and selling—we focus on understanding and successfully managing the myriad of different collaborative relationships that enable an organization to prosper. For today prospering is not simply a matter of picking the right strategies for one organization, but picking the right strategies *and* the right organizations to collaborate with, in order to achieve them. It is a new strategic challenge: that of developing the organizational ecosystem that has just the right components to support your aims, at just the right point in time, and then successfully maintaining that ecosystem's health and vitality.

Appreciating the art of collaborative working

If you have experienced the frustration, wasted time and cost of a failed collaborative effort, you will know that there is significant skill involved in making collaborative working successful. But because of our collective failure to recognize the connected nature of the organizational world, we have, to date, largely failed to educate managers and leaders sufficiently in the art of making collaborative working effective. This book aims to help redress this balance, exploring the full spectrum of collaborative working issues, from strategic decision-making about whether to collaborate, to the nitty-gritty practicalities of making it work once you have embarked on it.

We start with a conceptual framework in Chapter 1 that aims to clear some of the fog away from the term "collaboration," and which explores some of the language and labels that surround cross-organizational working. Out of the wealth of approaches to collaboration, across every sector, we identify the core themes and the key activities that will face you no matter what type of collaboration you embark upon. We continue in Chapters 2 through 9 looking at each of these core themes and activities, sharing some of the key lessons learnt in practice from a range of organizations that have been immersed in the day-to-day realities of collaborative working. These lessons are structured under these primary headings:

Chapter 2:   Preparing to collaborate—choosing when, how and with whom.

Chapter 3:   Structuring collaborative work—exploring the options for governance structures.

Chapter 4:   Integrating the team and agreeing joint outcomes—developing strong personal relationships and committing to a shared vision and goals.

Chapter 5:   Nurturing the collaborative process—stakeholder management, consensus-building, conflict resolution.

Chapter 6:   Resourcing the collaborative effort—ensuring you have the money and people to achieve the results you want.

Chapter 7:   Communicating and sharing information—keeping people connected between face-to-face meetings and sharing information, including dealing with the thorny issue of intellectual property.

Chapter 8:   Learning from experience—developing a continuous improvement culture and evaluating the return on investment in collaboration.

Chapter 9:   Collaborative skills, leadership and specialist roles—focusing on the unique capability profiles required for working across organizational boundaries.

Chapter 10 focuses on the challenges of internal collaboration, something that often proves as challenging as external collaboration for many organizations. The premise put forward in this chapter is that becoming skilled at working across internal boundaries is excellent preparation—and possibly a precondition—for working well with external partners.

Finally, in Chapter 11 we reflect on the lessons emerging from the experiences of organizations that have been grappling with this multifaceted challenge, and consider how you might enhance your own organization's capability to achieve collaborative advantage.

Please note that this relatively logical sequence of chapters does not mean that the book must be read like a novel, from beginning to end. Chapters 1 and 2 are probably useful, as they set the context for the remaining chapters. After that, depending on the issues that you are facing, you may wish to target and read specific chapters, each of which includes a number of real-life examples from around the world to illustrate key points, and a summary checklist of important questions to consider. As a fellow practitioner, I am only too aware of the difficulty of finding enough time to read and reflect. I hope this modular format— and the liberal sprinkling of practical examples—will make it as enjoyable and efficient a process as possible for you.

1 Developing a Common Language

In order to take effective action in any situation, a conceptual grasp of the task at hand is essential. Imagine trying to drive a car when you have no understanding of the rules of the road—what green, yellow or red traffic lights mean, why there are white lines down the middle of the road, or what the metal signs with numbers on them signify. You may be able to operate the vehicle but the outcome is still likely to be a disaster. Learning to operate in a collaborative, networked world has some similarities with the rather disconcerting situation just described. There are effective and less effective ways of operating; there are important guidelines to follow, but to date these have been implicit rather than explicit, generally discovered by trial and error rather than through education or training.

It is time to put this right and give the many people involved in collaborative work a more useful map of the territory. There is now a great deal of experience in cross-organizational working, in all sectors and every country around the world, which can help to draw the contours of the map. However, just as there is no one right way of driving a car, there is no one right way of facilitating collaborative work. The actions you choose to take will depend very much on the particular circumstances in which you find yourself. Nonetheless, some clear common themes emerge when one listens to the experiences of people who have spent time in collaboration with others. So let us explore the territory of collaborative working. In this chapter, we start by considering some of the language that is used in relation to the topic, and develop a framework to give some shape to a broad, multi-faceted field. Then, speaking something closer to a common language, we explore the key practical actions that help to increase the chances of collaborative success, in the chapters that follow.

The importance of language

An enormous range of terms is used to describe collaborative working between different organizations. Here is a selection of some of the most commonly used labels:

▶ alliance
▶ partnership
▶ network
▶ coalition
▶ co-operative
▶ consortium
▶ group
▶ virtual corporation
▶ extended enterprise
▶ association
▶ community
▶ joint venture
▶ collaborative
▶ federation
▶ forum
▶ collective
▶ constellation.

Adding to the confusion generated by such a multitude of labels, different organizations define these terms differently—one organization's "consortium" may be another's "network." Some of these arrangements will be established as formal legal entities, others will be much more informal processes of meeting, talking, and taking action together. Some will involve only two organizations; others may involve dozens of organizations. Some are created to deliver one specific outcome, others have a long-term focus and tackle many different projects as relationships and ideas evolve. Some are coordinated by one or more of the partner organizations; others are supported by a formal coordination mechanism, with its own staff and budget. With collaboration taking so many different forms, are there useful lessons that can be shared, from one type of collaborative venture to another?

The simple answer is yes. Two common factors underpin all collaborative processes between organizations: the need for individual human beings to engage successfully with one another, and the need for their organizations to engage effectively with them and with the collaborative process. Since every type of organizational collaboration must address these two issues, it follows that many lessons will be transferable from one collaborative process to another.

We shall explore the common traits of all forms of organizational collaboration, seeking the essence of what makes collaboration effective while accepting that different organizations will apply a wide range of labels to the process, and choose many different structures and approaches. We shall identify the critical success factors that underpin the many forms of partnership, and ensure that you know which questions to ask your own organization before embarking on a collaborative journey.

Defining collaborative advantage

Let us start with the basic tenets on which all subsequent chapters are based. First of all, this is the definition of "collaborative advantage" from which everything else flows.

COLLABORATIVE ADVANTAGE

The benefits achieved when an organization accomplishes more than it would have independently, by developing effective working relationships with other organizations.

This definition describes the outcome one aims to achieve. However, because every human interaction can potentially be defined as a form of collaboration, we need to define the term "collaboration" more specifically. Here are three key distinctions, which define the scope of collaboration more precisely, for the particular context and purpose of this book.

DISTINCTION 1: ORGANIZATIONS WORKING TOGETHER TO ACHIEVE ONE OR MORE SPECIFIC OUTCOMES

We are placing the spotlight on a form of interaction that involves different organizations working together. Of course individuals collaborate: neighbors work together to hold their annual street party, church members work together to raise money for local charities, Internet discussion group members offer help and advice to other group members. Here, however, we focus on the particular kind of collaboration where at least two organizations work together—represented, of course, by individuals, but nonetheless participating in the collaborative effort as organizations. This distinction is important because although many of the key success factors, as we shall see, relate to the development of relationships between individuals, there is always an organizational perspective that needs equal—or sometimes even greater—focus and attention.

Organizations have many opportunities to connect with each other, for example through a whole range of networks and associations, many of which are fora for sharing ideas and making new contacts. Valuable though these processes may be, they do not fit our definition of true collaboration, as they do not require organizations to agree on a joint outcome, or to build the foundation of trust that enables effective joint working. However, participation in such networks is often the catalyst for one or more organizations deciding to collaborate for a particular purpose, as we discuss in more detail in Chapter 2. At the point of making the decision to work jointly towards a common aim, they then fit our definition of collaboration. For example, let us envisage a situation where the chief executives of a number of businesses meet at a public management development program at a leading business school. That in itself is not truly a collaborative effort, although people from different organizations are meeting and learning together. However, let us say that at that program, several of the organizations agree to pilot a process of board member exchanges, thus building the capability of their respective boards. This process, designed with a specific outcome in mind and managed by the organizations themselves, fits our definition of inter-organizational collaboration, and may help each of the participating organizations to achieve collaborative advantage.

So our exploration of critical success factors will home in specifically on what it takes for organizations to achieve joint outcomes. This goes beyond simply interacting with other organizations.

DISTINCTION 2: ACTIONS NOT JUST WORDS

There has been a tendency in recent years to apply terms like "partnership working" to customer–supplier relationships and other transactional relationships. More often than not, this proves to be lip service rather than a truly transformed way of working. A purely contractual relationship, where one party has much greater economic power than the other, cannot in our terms be a true collaborative relationship. We focus primarily on those relationships where power is more evenly distributed, risk is shared, and where the parties involved are committed to a joint outcome, not simply an economic transaction. Some of the innovations in the automobile manufacturing industry, for example, where the relationship between supply chain members has been redefined to enable them to operate as true partners—working towards a common benefit and with shared risks and rewards—would qualify as collaborative working in our terms.[1] However, a government department relabeling its IT outsourcing provider as a "partner" while retaining all of the traditional customer–supplier processes—invitations to tender, service level agreements, contract change control processes—is not truly embarking on a collaborative effort as we define it here. There may well be lessons from true collaborative working that can improve such traditional relationships, but we shall be making the case that true collaboration differs in a number of significant ways from traditional commercial relationships. Collaborative working cannot be made to happen simply by calling it such—the right aims, attitudes, behaviors, processes, and resources need to be in place to make it a reality.

DISTINCTION 3: COLLABORATIVE LEADERSHIP AND CONSENSUS-BUILDING

Unlike traditional hierarchies, a collaborative effort has distributed leadership and a fundamentally egalitarian approach to action. Consensus building lies at its heart. Although it is possible that a hierarchy of authority may be in place, such as the position of authority held by the chief executive of a joint venture company, we would nonetheless maintain that if one partner in particular has the final say in every decision, once again this is not true collaboration as we are defining it.

In a true collaborative effort, it is difficult to distinguish between leading it and participating in it. The two roles intertwine, with different organizations or individuals taking the lead at different times on different issues. In Chapter 9, we explore how collaborative leadership is different from hierarchical leadership, and how to assess the readiness of your own organization to work collaboratively.

In summary, the lessons that you will read in the chapters to come, provided by a wide range of different organizations from the private, public, and voluntary sectors, apply to experiences where these organizations have chosen to collaborate with other organizations, put real investment into it, and learnt to make things happen in an environment where they can influence but not control.

The reasons organizations collaborate

Much of the literature on this subject describes alliancing and partnerships in terms of their characteristics. For example, you will read that organizations collaborate in order to access skills that they do not possess—sometime termed co-specialization—or that they collaborate with competitors in order to neutralize them as threats—sometime called co-option or co-optition.[2] Although these distinctions are useful, the

drawback of describing collaboration in terms of its qualities or characteristics is that this does not help you make that initial decision to
collaborate. In other words, rather than outlining the defining characteristics of collaboration, it might be more useful to define what
collaboration is for. Which outcomes might you achieve better through
collaboration?

We would therefore like to offer an initial conceptual map that is
focused on outcomes rather than characteristics. We have identified eight
principal outcomes that organizations often choose to achieve through
collaboration. These are as follows.

EIGHT PRINCIPAL REASONS TO COLLABORATE

1. **More effective research.**
2. **Greater influence.**
3. **Increased probability of winning business.**
4. **Faster, better, or cheaper development of products, services or markets.**
5. **Faster, better, or cheaper delivery of products or services.**
6. **In-depth learning.**
7. **Meeting an external requirement.**
8. **Saving costs.**

We now explore each of these in turn.

RESEARCH

Organizations explore new research areas in collaboration with
others, in order to gain access to the widest possible spectrum of
ideas, contacts, and experience. Not surprisingly, you will often find
a mixture of industry and academic partners involved in research
efforts, often with participation from public sector partners as well.
The European Commission, for example, is well known for funding
significant research programs, sometimes stretching over many years,
involving research consortia that can have dozens of members. One
of the European Commission project officers working on research
into collaboration technologies within the European Information
Society Technologies (IST) program, Paul Hearn, commented:

The best collaborative research projects are often ones in which the team members can let go of their own (sometimes entrenched) views and ideas, and apply a different, more open style of working with others. This is more difficult than it seems! Some of the best collaborative colleagues are those that can "leave their ego at the door," not always have to be right. Sometimes even in research projects on the topic of collaboration itself, the quality of collaboration within the team is sub optimal. How often do we see repeated attempts by an individual to validate his or her pet framework or idea, at the cost of disenfranchising others or inviting them into a zero-sum game! Instead collaboration is an opportunity to move beyond our own views, to contribute to new thinking—thinking which is truly a product of the group experience and not the individual experience. Ultimately, people's contribution to collaborative research should be judged on the basis of what they contribute to this wider process itself, not on their past experiences, their status or on how loudly or vociferously they hold to a position or view, especially when it is to the detriment of the group moving to a higher level or achieving broader goals.

Research projects often cross geographic as well as organizational boundaries, as in the case of the UK–Japan Collaboration on Climate Change Science, which was launched at the British Embassy in Tokyo in January 2005. UK and Japanese scientists are working together to advance the science of predicting climate change. The five-year partnership involves six scientists from the NCAS Centre for Global Atmospheric Modelling (CGAM) and the Met Office's Hadley Centre being based in Japan where they will have access to the Japanese Earth Simulator supercomputer, one of the world's most powerful machines. The UK scientists bring their experience of state-of-the-art climate models.

Collaborative research will sometimes be limited to research outcomes only, and in other cases will extend to the development of products and services resulting from that research.

INFLUENCING

It is sometimes much more powerful to be able to say "we" rather than "I." When you identify a need to influence others—say a national government or a standards-setting body—there is only so much influence that one organization can bring to bear. Many industries have spawned influencing bodies, sometimes assembled to fight one particular cause, but more often than not put in place to lobby on different issues over time. In such influencing processes, the participants are often competitors in every other setting but this one. Here are just a few examples:

▶ The Scotch Whisky Association has a membership of every whisky distiller in Scotland. Although they are competitors, they see the value of collaborating via the mechanism of this association, in order to protect their collective brand name of whisky and promote their products worldwide.[3]
▶ The European Low Fares Airline Association has 11 European low-fare airlines as members, and its aims are "to ensure that European policy and legislation promote free and equal competition to enable the continued growth and development of low fares into the future, allowing a greater number of people to travel by air."[4]
▶ The National Cotton Council (NCC) in the United States aims to ensure that the different segments of the US cotton industry—producers, warehousers, ginners, cottonseed, cooperatives, merchants, and manufacturers—can compete profitably and effectively at home and abroad, and works with government to represent the industry's interests. Six program committees make recommendations to the Board of the Council, but resolutions are only adopted following a voting process with the NCC delegates.[5]

In some cases, significant infrastructure is put in place to support lobbying efforts—organizations such as the Confederation of British Industry in the United Kingdom or the US Chamber of Commerce are well known for championing particular causes for the benefit of the wider business community, such as taxation or employment legislation proposals. Although joining such organizations is worth consideration as part of the process of developing your own organization's collaborative advantage, we would again argue that your collaborative capability is only truly put to the test when you make a conscious decision to join with a specific number of other organizations to influence on a particular issue. For example, the American Bureau of Shipping, Norwegian Det Norske Veritas and UK-based Lloyd's Register are all in the business of setting technical standards for ships and registering ships against them. The three organizations took a significant step in 2001 when they decided to collaborate on technical design rule sets for oil tankers and bulk carriers. By collaborating in order to agree a common set of standards, they were making a conscious choice to make the lives of their customers—shipbuilders and owners—much easier. Rather than competing on the basis of different technical standards, they chose to collaborate on the standards while continuing to compete in terms of customer service. This was a step change for their industry, which challenged the way things were done, to the benefit of their customers.

Collaborating with others—sometimes competitors, sometimes not—to influence more successfully is one of the opportunities to gain collaborative advantage.

INCREASED PROBABILITY OF WINNING BUSINESS

Every organization makes strategic choices about the capabilities, products, and services that it will develop. Inevitably there will be gaps in what it can offer to potential customers. The great power of collaborative advantage is that it opens many new avenues, giving organizations the opportunity to join forces with others who plug the gaps in their own portfolio. Sometimes partners brings specific skills, products, or services to the party. Sometimes they bring less tangible advantages, such as the doors they can open or the power of their brand in the marketplace.

UK-based consultancy TFPL, which specializes in knowledge and information management, identified an opportunity to develop an e-learning product aimed at increasing information literacy skills across large organizations. TFPL had all of the required content knowledge but not the technical capability to develop the actual software product. Based on agreed criteria, they identified a number of potential software development partners and discussed the possibility of collaboration with several of them. A small software development company was found to be a good fit, both strategically and culturally, and the two companies went on to produce a successful product. Because of the good fit and solid working relationship between the two firms, the relationship developed into a number of other joint client proposals.

In today's connected world, there is no longer any reason to feel constrained by the limits of your own organization's capability. By collaborating with others, you can create an exact match—or something very close to it—for what your customer requires.

FASTER, BETTER, OR CHEAPER DEVELOPMENT OF PRODUCTS, SERVICES, OR MARKETS

Collaborating in order to develop something better, faster, or cheaper—which you may then market separately or jointly—is increasingly common. The automobile industry has seen the benefits of collaborating in this way, the collaboration between Peugeot Citroen and Mitsubishi to develop a 4x4 being just one example. In the pharmaceutical industry, smaller biotechnology firms and global pharmaceutical players often collaborate on new drug development. In the oil industry, competitors work together to develop oil fields that they could not afford to develop independently. Choosing to create joint intellectual property or other assets with competitors, and shifting your competitive advantage to other areas such as marketing and distribution, is a key aspect of developing collaborative advantage—in other words, spotting the part of your business process that will give you greater benefit if undertaken with others, while still maintaining your overall competitive advantage through other aspects of the value chain.

In other cases, the collaboration is not between competitors but rather between companies with complementary skills. Here are just a few samples:

▶ Electrical goods company Philips worked together with Dutch coffee manufacturer Douwe Egberts to create a new coffee machine called the Senseo. Philips manufactures the machines and Douwe Egberts makes the coffee pads used in the machines. The two companies brought complementary knowledge to the process and the result was an innovative new product.
▶ International designer Starck teamed with sportswear company Puma to create a unique range of casual shoes. The two company logos feature equally on the website advertising the shoe (www.starck.puma.com), and both organizations promote the benefits of their partnership.
▶ Swiss retailer Migros teamed up with online retailer LeShop.com in order to make a more rapid transition into the world of online shopping, rather than building up the online capability itself.

When companies look to enter new geographic markets, the process of implementation can be significantly accelerated by partnering with a local firm that is immersed in the culture, language, and idiosyncrasies of that particular market. The dramatic number of partnerships now in place to develop business in China are but one example of this approach.

The challenge of building collaborative advantage under this broad heading is largely one of creativity—having the imagination to find and work with partners your competitors might never have even considered.

DELIVERING PRODUCTS AND SERVICES

In many sectors, organizations can only deliver what their stakeholders require by collaborating with others. Large information technology infrastructure outsourcing deals, for example, often require a consortium of partners for delivery. Competing private equity firms sometimes have to band together to finance deals that require their joint financing ability. Major civil engineering projects, large housing developments, significant events such as the Olympics—none of these can be delivered by one single organization. In this area, there is an overlap between traditional contractual relationships—between prime contractors and sub-contractors, for example—and collaborative ones. However, a collaborative approach is the only way to succeed on these demanding initiatives. The adversarial relationships that existed in the past between different delivery organizations serving the same customer—the construction industry has suffered from this, for example—often led to major budget and time overruns as well as legal wranglings. Approaching joint delivery with a view to achieving collaborative advantage means rethinking the process completely and finding the win–win for all involved, with the ultimate client's needs remaining at the forefront.

Different aspects of delivery can be handled collaboratively. For example, in the drinks industry, four companies decided they would gain collaborative advantage by marketing and distributing their products jointly, in all markets outside the United States. The four shareholders of joint venture company Maxxium, each with a 25 percent stake, are:

▶ Jim Beam Brands Worldwide, Inc., headquartered in Chicago, Illinois, USA.
▶ V&S Group (owners of Absolut Vodka), headquartered in Stockholm, Sweden, owned by the Government of Sweden.
▶ The Edrington Group, headquartered in Glasgow, Scotland's leading independent Scotch whisky group and owners of the Famous Grouse whisky brand.
▶ Rémy Cointreau SA, headquartered in Paris, France, owners of Rémy Martin cognac and Cointreau.

Maxxium gives these companies an efficient route to market, with greater economies of scale and global reach than would otherwise have been possible. Commenting on the model they have chosen, Maxxium's Director of Strategy and Development Arnaud Lodeizen says:

> *The driver for the creation of Maxxium was the merger that created market leader Diageo. If we hadn't pulled together, none of us would have independently reached the market position that Maxxium is now in. We are a non-integrated company, meaning we have a great deal of flexibility and empowerment to balance global brand requirements with local market knowledge. But it does mean needing to be able to handle a great deal of complexity and build strong relationships with a wide range of stakeholders.*

Have you considered which aspects of delivering your products or services could be better achieved working collaboratively?

LEARNING

Learning takes place at many levels when organizations collaborate. It is an inevitable consequence of working with others, although some organizations are better at exploiting the learning than others. However, in some cases learning itself is the specific objective. Many benchmarking processes involve collaboration between different organizations, for example. Some companies choose to work together to educate their managers. At Solvay Business School in Brussels, a consortium of five specialized financial services firms brings a number of their managers together several times a year to build their strategic business management capability. Called the Transconstellation Academy, it is a collaborative approach to learning. Why invest in the additional time and effort required to agree a joint curriculum? Paul Verdin, Chair in Strategy and Organization at Solvay Business School in Brussels and Visiting Professor at INSEAD, who is co-director for the Transconstellation Academy, says:

> *All of the partners in the Academy recognize that there is more learning that comes from a programme involving different companies in the same business. They get to see issues from a range of different perspectives. The partners also build relationships that may be useful to them in other ways. The Academy offers a concrete opportunity for all the companies involved, by meeting on a regular basis and at the highest level, to join their energies to create a strong lobby and increase the visibility of the sector.*

Business schools and other higher education institutions are not the only facilitators of collaborative learning programs. In the local government sector in the United Kingdom, an agency known as the Improvement and Development Agency for Local Government (IdeA) was set up to help facilitate best practice sharing between different local authorities. They put in place a number of collaborative processes that enabled different authorities to learn from each other. For example, they designed and facilitated a number of consortia—called Accelerated Improvement Consortia—which brought ten or so authorities together over a six-month period to share their ideas and experiences around particular performance improvement issues. The IdeA provided process facilitation and resource investigation, enabling the authorities involved to concentrate on productive learning discussions when they met.

As the ability to learn faster than your competitors is often cited as one of the keys to competitive advantage, have you considered how collaboration with other organizations might make a contribution to this?

MEETING AN EXTERNAL REQUIREMENT

In a number of cases, organizations have no choice but to collaborate. In the UK public sector, for example, local councils are required to establish local strategic partnerships (LSPs) which bring together the key organizations serving a community (local government, health, police, fire and rescue, voluntary organizations, local businesses) to define and deliver a community strategy. Although this makes sense on paper, it can be a real challenge to create a collaborative process that merges the interests of a very disparate group of organizations.

Similarly, a statutory obligation was placed on the UK police, fire, health, and local authorities to work together in the context of addressing crime and disorder in their local area. These Crime and Disorder Reduction Partnerships, which in 2005 numbered 376, also make a great deal of sense on paper—but only if the organizations involved have the skill necessary to make them effective.

In the commercial environment, organizations sometimes find themselves forced to collaborate with others in the context of delivering a particular product or service. A customer may have an established relationship with one or more suppliers, and award business on the condition that your organization works with one or more specific partners. Or in some cases, customers nervous about giving the entirety of a large project to one supplier will require collaboration between several suppliers, thus minimizing their reliance on one organization and spreading their risk. This can present particular challenges, as the imposed partners may well be competitors.

Imposed collaboration can be problematic as it generally eliminates partner choice, one of the critical success factors identified by many productive collaborative ventures. Nonetheless, there are still many factors which can be influenced and thereby increase the chance of achieving the desired outcomes. An executive coaching firm based in London, SKAI Associates, recognized the importance of partnership working for their clients and added the following paragraph to their client proposals:

> *Many of our clients like us to co-deliver with another supplier, or even two or three suppliers. We are very used to this too, and have acted as co-deliverer, party to a joint venture, consortium member, sub contractor, or lead deliverer marshalling other suppliers, on many occasions. Even if there is no defined contractual relationship, we always actively seek out our co-deliverer(s), to ensure seamless service and best practice.*

As SKAI has done, it is probably best to turn this possible threat into an opportunity.

SAVING COST

The ability to combine purchasing power has led to a number of collaborative approaches, often between competitors. For example, in the retail industry, 17 retailers from across the globe collaborated to establish the WorldWide Retail Exchange (WWRE), an online business-to-business exchange for retailers and suppliers. The WWRE enables greater economies of scale through consortium buying processes, and facilitates collaborative planning and forecasting between suppliers and retailers by giving them a common information platform and data set to work from. Spotting opportunities to save money by collaborating with others in this way—while being mindful of the risk of helping a competitor more than you have helped yourself—can have a very rapid bottom line impact, unlike other collaborative ventures which often need more time to bear fruit. The key investment of time, effort, and money goes into establishing the mechanism that will deliver the savings—whether it is an electronic tool such as an online auction or some other process. Once established, the collaborative process then becomes an operational one, requiring less of the ongoing investment in relationships that many other collaborative ventures require.

In Australia, the State Government of Victoria established a Community Sector Investment Fund. The purpose of this fund, administered by the Department of Human Services, was to help improve the efficiency of over 1200 non-government organizations providing services to the community. These Community Sector Organizations (CSOs) were offered funding to set up CSO Collaborative Networks to improve operational and administrative efficiency. The Department of Human Services set up an environment, a process, and a funding mechanism to enable the CSOs to explore where collaboration would result in a reduction in total time and/or costs across the collaborating entities. One of the opportunities that emerged, for example, was the possibility of streamlining the vehicle fleet management process across a number of CSOs' "networks." With the help of external advisors, a fleet management process was established which could be used by any CSO, leading to significant annual cost savings because of the increased economies of scale. Although this could also be viewed as an example of collaboration in response to an external requirement, it nonetheless exemplifies the significant gains that can be achieved by shared services—especially in the public sector, where organizations are not competing against each other in the market.

Looking across your sector, where could you save significant costs by combining forces with others? Often the only thing that stands in your way is the increasingly expensive mindset that everything you do must be controlled by people who work for you.

Multiple outcomes

Many collaborative ventures will of course aim at more than one of these eight outcomes. In the airline business, for example, a number of global alliances such as OneWorld, the Star Alliance, and SkyTeam have enabled groups of airlines to achieve a range of benefits:

▶ No one airline can serve every market. Alliances allow them to offer more routes to their customers.
▶ Alliances help boost an airline's growth by feeding passengers between members' networks.
▶ Airlines can achieve substantial savings by working more closely together and, for example, buying fuel jointly or sharing maintenance costs.
▶ Individual passengers and corporate customers value the benefits they get from alliances, such as being able to collect frequent flyer miles.

These benefits encompass a number of the outcomes we have covered, namely:

▶ increasing the probability of winning business
▶ delivering a better service
▶ developing new markets
▶ saving costs.

as well as a learning benefit where allied airlines share good practices between them. This is just one example of the breadth of benefits that can be achieved when organizations join together. A further benefit is that as certain airlines become more skilled at this form of global collaboration, those airlines that are not part of effective global groupings run the risk of significant loss of market share, due to weaker customer loyalty and higher costs. In the airline business, there is an increasingly clear divide between those airlines with collaborative advantage and those without.

The collaborative advantage radar

The eight outcome-focused headings can be used to assess whether your organization may be missing opportunities to achieve more by collaborating with others. One of the key aspects of 21st-century leadership is the ability to spot opportunities to gain collaborative advantage, and then to consider the costs and benefits of working with others versus going it alone. Having that collaborative radar, constantly scanning the horizon for useful collaborative opportunities, is an essential skill for the people involved in strategic decision-making processes. In order to assess whether your organization has an effective collaboration radar, you might like to discuss the following questions.

DO YOU HAVE A COLLABORATIVE ADVANTAGE RADAR?

▶ If you have a formal strategic planning process, are collaboration opportunities specifically reviewed as part of it?
▶ Do you keep track of the significant collaborative ventures in which your organization is engaged?
▶ If you have a competitive intelligence function, does it track what collaborations your competitors are involved in?
▶ Do any of your managers' job descriptions include responsibility for assessing collaboration opportunities? Is anyone dedicated to that task?
▶ Do any of your management development or training programs cover the topic of collaboration?

Spotting opportunities to collaborate is the first step along the much longer journey required to make a particular collaborative effort successful.

Risks, costs, and benefits

It is important to recognize that collaborative work requires significant resources and effort—and if the desired outcomes are not reached, it has just as much potential to disappoint as to delight your stakeholders.

It is therefore sensible to be mindful of the many potential pitfalls that await you as you embark upon this journey. Here are some of the key dangers to try to avoid:

▶ partner organizations with incompatible strategic and/or operational agendas
▶ partner organizations with incompatible cultures
▶ individual participants inexperienced or unskilled in collaborative work
▶ not enough political support in the organization for the collaborative agenda
▶ not enough time, money, or resources available to make it work
▶ personality conflicts and/or lack of trust between individual participants
▶ risk of contravening laws on anti-competitive behavior.

Any one of these issues can stand in the way of success—and more often than not, a number of these factors may be at play. Make no mistake about it: working collaboratively is not an easy option.

Yet set against these warnings is the potential for enormous benefit:

▶ credibility and effectiveness: the ability to win and/or deliver business by combining your own organization's skill set with others
▶ leverage: the ability to achieve key objectives beyond the capacity or capability of your own organization
▶ flexibility: the ability to move fast without needing to upsize or downsize your own organization
▶ cost savings: the ability to share costs with others while maximizing the return
▶ innovation: the ability to bring new ideas and perspectives onto your organizational challenges and achieve breakthroughs as a result.

For any collaborative process that you may be considering, just as for any other business decision, it is essential to carefully weigh up the risks and potential benefits and to make a judgment on whether to proceed. Some time spent doing this analysis before committing yourself will avoid the painful and costly process of extracting your organization from a collaborative process that never gets off the ground.

Where the effort is needed

We have already established that collaborative working takes many different forms. The experience of most organizations is that a collaborative venture has a number of aspects which need time and attention, whichever size, shape, or scope it has. The key activities can be summarized as follows:

KEY COLLABORATIVE ACTIVITIES

Preparing: identifying potential partners and discussing or testing joint working opportunities

Structuring: designing the most appropriate governance model

Integrating: creating an aligned team focused on common goals

Nurturing: protecting the health and vitality of the collaborative effort

Resourcing: ensuring the right resources are allocated to the right things

Communicating: building information flows to support the desired outcome(s)

Learning: reflecting on lessons learnt and sharing them within and beyond the collaborative venture.

These activities each have two major dimensions to them: the interpersonal aspect, in terms of the way that individuals within the collaboration relate to each other; and inter-organizational, the way in which each partner organization engages with that particular aspect of the collaborative process.

It is perhaps easier to understand the two dimensions of these seven activities by considering the key question(s) that apply to each of the dimensions. These can be summarized as shown in Table 1.1.

The ability to operate at both the inter-organizational and the interpersonal level simultaneously is one of the core skills involved in building collaborative advantage. Ventures that are successful at one level but not at the other are usually still doomed to failure.

Understanding the rules of the game

In the chapters to come we shall explore the different activities that form the core of collaborative working. Thanks to the contribution of individuals and

Table 1.1 **Inter-organizational and interpersonal challenges**

Activity	Inter-organizational	Interpersonal
Preparing	Who are the best partners for this venture, both strategically and operationally? Do our organizations have compatible cultures and ways of working?	Which individuals would we want involved in this venture? Can we work with this/these individual(s)? Do we have shared values?
Structuring	What is the best organizational and governance structure for what we are trying to achieve?	Which people are best suited to which roles?
Integrating	What are the common outcomes to which all partners are committed?	How do we build the trust required between the individuals involved?
Nurturing	Are the organizational sponsors of this initiative happy with its progress?	Are the individuals involved getting what they need and want out of it?
Resourcing	How will costs and benefits be allocated? Where will budgets and resources be held?	Who is accountable for what?
Communicating	Which communication and information-sharing processes need to be put in place?	Who needs to know what?
Learning	What return have we got from this investment?	How well are we working together?

organizations prepared to share their own experience and perspectives, we shall build a picture of what works and what doesn't, and gather tips and hints that can be applied at a practical level. However, if one practical lesson can be taken from this initial overview of what collaborative working is all about, it is perhaps that there is very little shared understanding of this complex—and growing—facet of organizational life. With the myriad of forms that collaborative working takes, the first significant step on this road may be to create your own organization's frame of reference for collaboration. Choose the language and frameworks that work for you and your company, integrate them into the right education processes—and make sure that the right people are engaged in understanding the territory. Only then will you be able to move to build your collaborative advantage—with everyone understanding the rules of the game they are playing.

2 Preparing to Collaborate

Given the effort required for successful cross-organizational collaboration, asking "Should we collaborate on this?" and then "With whom?" is important before embarking on the journey. We have already highlighted the pressure on resources and the ever-increasing expectations of stakeholders as the main drivers behind the quest to engage with partners. In the preceding chapter, we suggested eight major outcome-focused areas that hold the potential for achieving collaborative advantage. We outlined the seven principal activities that require significant effort and resources in order for collaborative work to have a successful outcome. However, most organizations with experience of collaborative work emphasize the fundamental importance of the preparation phase, and in particular the importance of picking the right partner(s).

The ability to judge whether there is an opportunity to gain collaborative advantage is one that develops with experience, and depends on many different variables. However a possible first step on the road is to gain an understanding of the collaborative relationships your organization already has.

The relationship audit

It is surprising how many organizations lack a complete picture of the relationships they have entered into with other organizations. Despite the significant investment that goes into these relationships, it is usually the case that no one is accountable for keeping an overview of the collaborative landscape for their organization. Finance directors keep track of the money, HR directors keep track of the people, but no one keeps track of the relationships with other organizations. As we discuss in a later chapter on roles and skills, this may well become an increasingly accepted role. In the meantime, it is likely that an efficient audit of what exists today will reveal where effective relationships have already been established. This is a worthwhile exercise, on the basis that it is much more efficient to build on existing relationships than to initiate new ones.

THE STORY OF THE BRITISH COUNCIL

The British Council, a non-profit, non-governmental organization charged with promoting British culture and educational opportunities outside the United Kingdom, had invested in a significant number of relationships in every one of the 110 countries in which it operates, since its ability to influence Is heavily dependent upon effective relationship-building at a local level. The British Council gave support to communities such as the English language teachers in each country by investing in newsletters and events to bring them together. In some countries they also established alumni associations for people who had the shared experience of attending academic institutions in Britain. In most places, they connected with other public, private, and civil society organiza-tions such as the ministries of education and arts bodies, and built relationships with wider communities through this route. They began to realize the strategic importance of their ability to influence and build relationships by investing or participating in local, regional, and in some cases global, networks. The British Council's outlook was very much one of building collaborative advantage and being able to extend their influence widely despite a relatively small number of employees (7000 worldwide).

Sue Maingay, country director for the British Council in Poland, asked her staff to complete an audit of all of the main networks and communities with which her country operation was engaged, regardless of the level of resource going in to each relationship and whether or not the network had been insti-gated by the British Council. She was astonished when the list came back with 52 different examples, for what was quite a small operation. She realized that as head of a country operation, it was important that she and her management team were aware of this wide range of relationships in order to determine how best to allocate the organization's limited resources. It was clear that some of the relationships were delivering more value than others, and having the list was a useful input to the organization's strategic planning process.

Sue Maingay says:

As a result of the exercise we realised that we were very good at establishing rela-tionships with active partners in ongoing projects, but not so good at maintaining those relationships once the project was completed. It is clear, however, that these networks represent a valuable resource for the achievement of future objectives— and one which we need to turn to better advantage. This does not need to involve massive extra resources. We do, however, need to be strategic in deciding which networks to maintain and develop, as well as clever and imaginative in how we plan to do this.

With relatively little investment of time, for example by using an email survey, you should be able to get a rapid picture of where the key relationships are today. This is important data as you prepare to consider further collaborative opportunities. An example of such an email is shown in the box.

SAMPLE RELATIONSHIP AUDIT

Dear Colleague,

As we are involved in an increasing number of collaborative arrangements across the company, I have been charged with pulling together a picture of our key relationships with other organizations. This information will be made available in a central database and will be kept up to date. Having this information will enable the whole company to support key relationships and develop them further. It will also enable us to quickly find key contacts for these relationships, as the database will also hold the contact details of the partnership managers.

Please complete the following template which should give us the basis for this important map of company activity.

Purpose of partnership
Start date (and end date if applicable)
Organizations involved and for each one, contact details for the partnership manager
Key benefits
Any other comments

Completing a brief questionnaire such as the one suggested is not a time-consuming task, and will form the basis of what should become a permanent knowledge base for the organization. A company would not lose track of the money in its bank accounts, nor should it lose track of the valuable relationships it has built up. Although a relationship may not be as tangible as cash, it is the result of significant investment. The relationship audit is likely to be useful at the level at which an overview of relationships has some meaning to the person analyzing it. An overview of every business relationship of a multi-national conglomerate will simply create information overload—but at the level of an operating business unit, it is likely to be important and useful data.

Making a strategic assessment

To assist the process of deciding whether to collaborate, it may be useful for the relevant stakeholders in your organization to discuss the following questions, in relation to the specific opportunity for collaboration:

DECIDING WHETHER TO COLLABORATE

▶ What is the outcome we are looking to achieve?
▶ What are the advantages and disadvantages of collaborating versus doing this ourselves?
▶ Who are the potential partners?
▶ What will each of them bring to the party?
▶ How will each of them benefit from the potential collaboration?
▶ Is there a good strategic and operational fit between our organization and theirs?
▶ How strong is our existing relationship with each?
▶ Is there a good cultural fit between our organization and theirs?
▶ What are the risks associated with this venture and how will we manage them?
▶ Is there an existing collaborative process that we could join rather than setting up a new one?
▶ How would we resource a potential collaboration?

A good discussion around these questions will enable you to make a first assessment of the potential for collaborative advantage. Cultural compatibility is an important consideration, according to those with a good track record of collaboration. An amusing example of this is suggested on the website advertising a range of designer shoes that resulted from a collaboration between international designer Starck and sportswear firm Puma. On their jointly branded website (www.starck.puma.com) advertising the range of shoes, they describe why the two firms decided to partner:

> *each with a passion for fun (a cheeky wink here, a practical joke there), a healthy disrespect for authority and a crazy belief that anything is possible, if you care enough to make it happen. Like lovers destined to cross paths, it was these irresistible desires that, in the end, brought them together.[1]*

Another interesting cultural mix can be found in the transnational strategic alliance between Honda and Disneyland Resort. Despite the significant differences between the two companies in terms of products and markets, the alliance was announced with an emphasis on cultural fit. Koichi Kondo, president and CEO, American Honda Motor Co., Inc., said, "This new alliance creates many new and exciting opportunities for both of our organizations. Our two companies hold a common belief in the importance of dreams,"[2] while Matt Ouimet, President of Disneyland Resort, stated, "We are thrilled to welcome Honda to the Disneyland Resort family. Honda is known throughout the world for quality, innovation and family values—qualities that our own founder, Walt Disney, instilled in Disneyland park 50 years ago."[3]

Shared values is one of the most important enablers to effective collaborative working. It may be possible to build shared values over time, but it is likely to be far more effective to collaborate with organizations that have similar values to begin with.

Exploring possibilities

Note that a "testing the waters" phase will be necessary once you have identified a possible collaboration opportunity. It is unrealistic to expect to leap from your own assessment of a collaboration opportunity to a detailed action plan, since in collaborative work the process of creating an alignment of goals with your partner organizations is key.

Here lies one of the major differences between running your own organization and collaborative work. The process of getting a collaborative venture underway is heavily loaded with investment of time and effort upfront, in a relationship-building, goal alignment phase. Whereas within your own organization you can make a strategic choice and allocate resources to make it happen, you do not hold that authority with a collaborative venture. You need to be prepared to allocate significant time to the exploration phase with your potential partners.

The decision to accomplish something collaboratively cannot truly be called a decision until all parties have signed up to it. At this early point in the process, it may be more appropriate to call it a decision to explore the possibility of collaboration with others. Taking this exploratory process seriously is important—handling it well can make the difference between success and failure, between a collaboration that is built on a solid foundation or sand.

Test and learn

It is often wise to consider testing a new collaborative relationship on a project that will not be too costly in money or reputation if it does not succeed. Because of the importance of strong personal relationships, trust, goal alignment and compatible working processes, a pilot project gives you the opportunity to assess the potential strength of that particular collaboration, with relatively little risk. As with a probation period for a new employee, it gives you the opportunity to get to know your partners much better. Should the pilot project be successful, it creates the foundation for future work together. If it is not successful, you are able to withdraw gracefully from the venture without suffering any wider negative impact.

Since implementation speed is an important aspect of competitive advantage, it is best to make a rapid assessment of collaboration potential and then get on with testing it. Otherwise there is the danger of a long delay as you complete complex risk assessments. Recognize that the only accurate way of assessing a collaborative relationship is to try it out, therefore testing the relationship is an important foundation for building collaborative advantage. As your organizational capability to assess partnerships develops, your ability to judge who will be an effective partner and who will not is likely to improve, and the whole process will become more efficient.

THE STORY OF THE BRITISH COUNCIL AND THE WORLD BANK INSTITUTE

The British Council and the World Bank established their strategic partnership in 1999. At first glance it might not be obvious why these two institutions decided to join forces. The British Council is charged with promoting one country's—the United Kingdom's—cultural and educational opportunities in other countries. With a turnover of around £500 million, its funding is dwarfed by the World Bank. The World Bank is a large, complex development bank which provides loans, policy advice, technical assistance, and knowledge-sharing services to the developing world. The partnership is more easily understood, however, when it becomes clear that it is the World Bank Institute, the part of the World Bank focused on a knowledge and learning agenda, that built the primary relationship with the British Council.

The two organizations had worked together on an *ad hoc* basis for some years, mainly in the form of the British Council carrying out World Bank-funded projects in a range of countries. The British Council has for many years had a member of its Washington office as a part-time relationship manager with the World Bank, keeping track of the World Bank's evolving priorities, and notifying British Council country directors of opportunities to bid for projects that would further both organizations' aims.

In 1997 the British Council identified that the UK government was developing a growing interest in the strategic importance of the knowledge economy. Aware of the World Bank's strategic shift from simply providing loans to also providing knowledge and learning services, it spotted an opportunity to join forces to improve both organizations' ability to act as a knowledge broker in different countries.

The British Council participated in a conference on the topic of knowledge for development, the Global Knowledge Conference, which took place in Toronto, Canada in the summer of 1997. The World Bank was a main organizer and sponsor of the event. The end result was a highly successful conference with over 2000 participants from 144 countries. Several months after the conference, a number of the participants, including the World Bank Institute and the British Council, decided to found an ongoing community to continue to develop the ideas and actions around the knowledge for development agenda, which they named the Global Knowledge Partnership. Through their contacts on this initiative, the British Council and the World Bank Institute found there was a meeting of minds, a commitment to the same aims and ideals, as well as easy working relationships. This eventually led to a Memorandum of Understanding being signed between the two organizations in 1999, in which they agreed to seek opportunities to collaborate and learn from each other in a number of areas, including but not limited to knowledge for development. A partnership manager was appointed on both sides, and the partnership continues to this day, having resulted in a number of cross-organizational learning initiatives and joint projects.

This last example shows how relatively small joint projects can open the way to a more formal and significant alliance. Sometimes this evolution is unplanned, part of the natural development of ongoing activities, but it can equally start with a conscious decision to test a potential long-term collaborative relationship.

Finding potential partners

If you have a very specific objective in mind, you may decide to take a structured, strategic approach to finding potential partners, involving a clear list of criteria and formal research to identify the organizations that meet those criteria. However, in many cases collaboration opportunities simply emerge from existing relationships, developed from a conversation over dinner or an interesting discussion at a conference. To draw an analogy, single people looking for a relationship are generally encouraged to get out there and participate in a whole range of activities to increase their chances of finding a mate. The same challenge should be put to organizations wishing to build collaborative advantage. It is important to get out there, join professional groups that are doing interesting things, and build relationships with other organizations which may start as informal contacts, but over time become serious collaborative efforts. There is such a wide variety of these sorts of networks, serving every possible professional interest, that each organization will have to make its own assessment as to which ones are worth joining. There are professional associations, influencing groups, dinner clubs of senior executives, benchmarking clubs, management development consortia, local Chamber of Commerce activities, alumni groups, charitable foundations, discussion groups sponsored by commercial firms, even sport clubs and cultural activities—any number of opportunities to get to know other organizations.

The following questions might be useful in choosing which ones to join, bearing in mind that some of these networks and clubs involve some quite significant membership fees.

WHICH NETWORKS SHOULD WE JOIN?

▶ Is the purpose of this network useful to us, even if it doesn't lead to any collaboration opportunities?

▶ Which other organizations are members and are they interesting organizations for us to meet?

▶ Who represents their organizations in this network, and are those individuals useful for us to meet?

▶ What do existing members think of the services and events offered by this network?

▶ How many people would we involve in this particular network and how might this benefit them personally?

▶ What are the membership costs and do they represent good value for money?

Participating in these networks generally does not require much time and effort, as someone will be responsible for organizing the networking processes for you. All that is generally required is payment of membership fees, and participation in the events hosted by the network organizer. To give a better sense of how participating in such networks can lead to real, outcome-focused collaboration, let us consider the story of two very different networks: the Family Business Network, with 1800 members in 50 countries, and the Cambridge Network, with approximately 1000 members all based in one region.

THE STORY OF THE FAMILY BUSINESS NETWORK

The Family Business Network (FBN) was founded in 1990 with an expressed aim of increasing the quality of leadership and management of family-owned enterprises. It is global in scope, covering over 50 countries. It is in effect a federation of local chapters, which organize local and regional events, as well as meeting annually for a global conference which is organized centrally. FBN is set up as an independent not-for-profit association to provide educational and networking opportunities for family businesses, and is headquartered in Lausanne, Switzerland.

Professor Joachim Schwass, a professor at the international business school IMD, one of the network's sponsor organizations, is an FBN board member and was executive director of FBN for ten years. He describes the process he observes most members following when they join the network:

Initially family businesses join out of curiosity, somewhat non-committally. They wonder if they might learn something but their objectives are very loose. Then when they find they do learn some useful things at Network events, their commitment and interest grows. They then start to apply some of the learning in their own organization. For example, family businesses who might only have had informal communication processes learn of the benefit of formalising a Family Council process and go back to try that out in their own company. What we have also seen is people meeting at FBN events and some real business collaboration resulting from it.

THE STORY OF THE CAMBRIDGE NETWORK

The Cambridge Network has a much more limited scope geographically than the Family Business Network, but an equally impressive number of members. The idea for the Cambridge Network germinated at a dinner in 1998, when six well-known figures from six different worlds—academia, high tech, life sciences, venture capital, investment banking, accountancy—found themselves bemoaning the fact that despite its international brand recognition, Cambridge as a city-state seemed to be punching below its weight. Despite a number of very influential and interesting communities being present in Cambridge, such as the academic community and the high-tech research community, there was relatively little contact between them. The six "heroes," as network managing director Peter Hewkin describes them, decided this was something that they might actually be able to influence if they pooled their respective expertise and personal networks, and worked together to develop opportunities for organizations based in Cambridge.

As a first step they asked someone to research good practices across the globe in terms of promoting a city-state. The benchmark this person identified was an initiative called San Diego Connect, which had started within San Diego University but had broadened out to encompass a whole range of stakeholders from the San Diego area. The Cambridge team gleaned as much as possible from the San Diego approach and then set up a limited company called the Cambridge Network. The expressed aim of the Cambridge Network is as follows:

The Cambridge Network aims to create and support a community of like-minded people from business and academia in the Cambridge region and link this community to the global high-tech network for the benefit of the Cambridge region. The Cambridge Network enables its members to work together and leverage their collective resources in new ways for the benefit of technology-enabled enterprise and adjacent stakeholders in the Cambridge region. We achieve this by using a variety of technology, knowledge and people-based tools to enhance business processes on both a local and a global scale.[4]

The six founding members engaged a further 20 founder members through their personal reputations and influence. These founder members control four elected seats on the board. Since the network's inception, a further 1000 organizations have joined the network and participate in its special interest group discussions, social events, conferences, and study tours. They also elect a "Young Turk" member of the board. The network is self-funding and has chosen not to seek government funding, in order to preserve its independence.

One collaborative idea that emerged from a Cambridge Network meeting was the idea of making training and development a more efficient process for network members. The organizations that chose to participate shared information about their repective in-house training programs, and offered any spare places to other Cambridge companies that might benefit from that training. Called The Learning Collaboration (TLC), this developed as a sub-community of the Cambridge Network, with 40 different organizations signing up to participate. The Cambridge Network gave TLC some space on their website and generally encouraged the group's development. Without the introductions made possible by the Cambridge Network, this innovative collaboration would probably never have happened.

Serendipity

Joining associations and networks is undoubtedly useful for relationship-building, but there is also no doubt that many collaborative ventures come from purely serendipitous encounters. A classic example of one such development follows.

A STORY ABOUT TACKLING AIDS

Geoff Parcell, a senior advisor at energy company BP, recounts the story of a fascinating collaboration that emerged as a result of a number of people meeting at a workshop in Thailand in 2003. Geoff had been seconded by BP to UNAIDS, an arm of the United Nations set up to coordinate the UN's efforts in addressing the AIDS epidemic. Geoff had been heavily involved in BP's efforts to mobilize knowledge across the company, and had co-authored a book on the tools and techniques that he and his colleagues had used.[5] It was felt that his experience was directly relevant to building awareness about handling the prevention and spread of AIDS. Geoff found himself at a workshop in Chiang Mai in northern Thailand, organized by the University of Chiang Mai AIDS education program, where he met a very diverse group of people. They were brought together by their interest in tackling AIDS and their belief that the best way to do so was to help people find their own solutions. The workshop covered the BP knowledge management experience, the Salvation Army's approach to helping others to help themselves, UNAID's experience from around the world and Thailand's experience of reducing HIV by tackling it in the community. The people who attended the event were struck by some of the connections between their experiences, and undertook to go away and think through how they could combine their skills and knowledge to really make a difference to people living with AIDS.

The end result of that period of consideration, with the individuals concerned spread out across six countries, was a simple one-page self-assessment tool which invited users to assess themselves against ten practices that the participants in Chiang Mai had experienced as important in reducing the incidence of AIDS. The idea was that people could identify where they were strong and where they had something to learn, and who they could learn from. The team tried the approach in a few villages in Uganda and Kenya, and having achieved some success, moved it into Brazil where a consortium of 15 cities signed up to use the approach.

The Brazilian experience was so successful that the team, with sponsorship from the United Nations Institute for Training and Research (UNITAR), then held a global conference to give participants the opportunity to instantly share knowledge and experience around the issues. Fourteen cities from around the globe, from Bombay to Bangkok, to Lyon and Gothenburg, were invited to send representatives. Each city team had to include representatives from local government, NGOs tackling AIDS and people living with AIDS. The event was held in October 2003 in Lyon, and was structured as a series of round table discussions, based on what people had to offer and what they wanted to know. Geoff Parcell observed:

When the representatives from Burkina Faso shared their experience of testing migrant workers for AIDS and how they handled that process, the representatives from Lyon were taking copious notes. I know for a fact that just seeing other people—

and from a place as far away as Lyon no less—taking an interest in what they had done will have made the Burkina Faso team redouble their efforts when they got home.

The success of the Lyon event motivated the team to take on an even greater challenge. They put on an even bigger event in Chiang Mai in July 2004 which they called the Knowledge Fair on AIDS. A hundred and forty people from 30 countries attended. For this Knowledge Fair, the team set up a structure of ten different rooms covering the ten major good practice areas, and people circulated between them, picking up the knowledge they needed and sharing the knowledge they had. Each participant came up with five concrete things he or she could do to improve local practices. Again, the feedback was hugely positive.

These ambitious, global initiatives were the result of a collaboration between a group of committed individuals who, with the support of their organizations, decided to take on a big challenge. The UNAIDS unit and the Salvation Army formalized a partnership in support of this work, but otherwise it was an informal arrangement, with funding coming from a range of sources. This informal arrangement is now evolving into a networked organization called the Constellation for AIDS Competence. A company has been set up in Belgium, with a secretariat in Chiang Mai, with the original team members engaged in their organizational capacity or as independent consultants to the process. Who could have imagined, at that first meeting in Chiang Mai, that so much would emerge from that particular group of individuals and organizations finding themselves in one room?

Many collaborative ventures emerge in this unplanned way from the things that happen in day-to-day life. Being receptive to these possibilities—indeed actively seeking them out—is all part of the capability needed to build collaborative advantage.

Approaching potential partners

It is important to recognize that the exploratory phase of collaborative work is essentially a sales process. Your potential partners will need to sell their virtues to you, but you also need to be clear what you have to offer them. This is a particularly delicate process if you are approaching competitors as potential partners, for example in collaborating to deliver a product or service to customers. You need to divulge enough to assess the interest and potential of collaboration, but not so much that you find yourself at a competitive disadvantage if the collaboration does not progress.

Before you approach a potential partner, you may wish to consider completing a SWOT (strengths, weaknesses, opportunities, threats) analysis for that particular relationship. An illustration is given in the box.

A CASE STUDY TO CONSIDER

Imagine you work for a small graphic design company looking to win the business of producing the annual report of a major multinational. With a good local reputation in your own city but little reputation outside it, you are considering allying your company with another organization to increase the probability of winning the business. Your managing director mentions that he plays golf with the managing director of a communications consultancy which also produces annual reports for its clients. Your collaborative advantage radar picks up a possible opportunity, and you decide to assess the merits of that potential collaboration. Your SWOT analysis might look like Table 2.1.

Strengths (facts)	Weaknesses (facts)
▶ We have complementary skills ▶ Our CEOs already have a good personal relationship ▶ Our offices are close to each other so meeting will be easy	▶ We sometimes compete for business ▶ They have little experience of collaborative projects ▶ Neither of us have language translation capability
Opportunities (possible)	**Threats (possible)**
▶ Success on this project could lead to more business ▶ They have a stronger relationship with the customer than we do, so better chance to win ▶ Using their brand could give us much greater credibility in the market	▶ They might use what they learn about us to their advantage on other deals ▶ They have a stronger relationship with the customer so might not need us ▶ As they are a much larger company than us, they may not treat us as equals in the venture

Table 2.1 **SWOT analysis**
An example of a partner assessment

Having developed this analysis with some of your colleagues, you are then in a position to judge whether it is worth approaching the potential partner. Let us assume that you decide to make the approach. That initial approach is where first impressions are formed. It makes good sense to use existing relationships if they exist. In this case, the two managing directors know each other and play golf together. The first approach might well be one made in the clubhouse, at the end of a golf game. Although to some that may appear unprofessional, in practice it makes good business sense—the informal setting means no loss of face if there is no further progression, and it gives the potential partner time to reflect before moving to more formal discussions.

The next stage could be an exploratory meeting with the two managing directors and a few key staff members. For that first more formal meeting, you will need two key assets at your disposal: an agreed list of questions to put to the potential partner, and a clear outline of the benefits and risks of this particular partnership as you see them, for discussion.

Let us say that at that meeting you agree to bid for the piece of business together. At that point it may be useful to sign non-disclosure agreements to protect your intellectual property and any commercially sensitive information. The joint bidding process is in many ways a good test of the potential of the relationship: If that process does not go smoothly, it may be an indication that working together is not a viable option for either company. You will need to discuss branding issues, how the bid process will be managed, who will meet the client, how costs and income will be split should you win the business—all good tests of the collaborative process.

A joint bidding process such as this illustration should, all being well, enable key individuals within both companies to build a good working relationship and the beginnings of a foundation of trust. For this reason it is often most efficient to have the people involved in bidding for business collaboratively also leading on the implementation phase. Every positive relationship that is built in a collaborative setting should be treated as an asset. This means that continuity is important—changing the people involved can completely change the dynamics of the relationship. Every time a change of contributors is made, there should be a risk assessment of what damage (if any) it might do to the partnership.

Exploring options

The process of engaging with potential partners requires openness and flexibility. Although you may have a clear outcome in mind, your potential partner will inevitably have a different perspective. They will have a different business context, a different set of personalities, a different landscape of power and politics. The early discussions need to be focused on identifying the wins for each partner in the venture. They should also put concerns and non-negotiable issues on the table. You may wish to consider inviting an external facilitator, someone who is not part of any of the partner organizations, to facilitate the exploratory discussions. This avoids the danger of anyone feeling that the process is being manipulated by a partner with a hidden agenda.

Clearly the more potential partners you involve in a collaborative venture, the more complex the exploratory phase becomes, with increasing scope for disagreement. It is often more practical to start with a smaller core of partners—maybe only two or three at the most—and then invite further contributors (if required) as the relationships evolve and it becomes clearer which additional skills and expertise are needed.

Agreeing an exit strategy

It may seem premature to agree an exit strategy when the collaborative venture is still in its design phase but in fact this is an important aspect of the preparation work. Imagine, for example, that two companies decide to deliver a particular range of services as a jointly branded package. Over time they build up a range of shared customers whose expectations are of continuing support from both organizations. If one organization then decides to pull out of the joint activity, what happens to those customers? What happens to the commitments already made to them? Rather than risking a raft of lawsuits and the loss of goodwill from angry customers, it is far better to anticipate the factors that could lead to the dissolution of a collaborative effort, and consider how these issues would be handled, in advance.

The most common issues to consider within an exit strategy are:

▶ customer service
▶ intellectual property rights
▶ branding issues
▶ compensation
▶ employee welfare
▶ what happens to joint assets.

Two professional service firms that were planning a collaboration even went so far as to appoint a mediator as part of their exit strategy planning, on the basis that if the collaboration fell apart unexpectedly, a mediator's skills would be useful. Luckily, they have yet to call on his services.

Naturally you will not be able to anticipate every circumstance, but a comprehensive discussion of an exit strategy at the set-up phase is likely to reduce the impact of one important risk factor in collaborative working—the risk that one or more partners withdraws.

Knowing your collaborative capacity

Collaborative working calls for specific skills and knowledge, and it is important to know who within your organization has the capability to collaborate effectively and act as your ambassador. The people who represent your organization in a collaboration will be the means by which strategic vision is turned into reality. In planning a collaborative venture, it is useful to know who you can call upon to participate in the venture, in whichever roles are required. As we discuss in more detail in Chapter 9, involving the right individuals in a collaborative venture is a critical success factor. A process for identifying and documenting collaborative experience and capability, in relation to specific individuals, will make it much easier to efficiently resource the partnerships that you decide to develop.

Planning for preparation

Preparing the ground for collaborating with others is an important and time-consuming task. In some ways it is a never-ending activity, if one looks at it as a kind of collaborative radar, constantly scanning the horizon for opportunities. Then, when a specific opportunity arises, it becomes a more focused dialogue between potential partners, exploring the risks and rewards of joining forces before formalizing the relationship. Some of these dialogues may lead to fruitful collaboration; others may not. Deciding when not to proceed—because the risks outweigh the potential rewards, for example—is just as important and valid a decision as deciding to move ahead. Having clear go/no go criteria will help ensure that you focus on the collaborative opportunities with the greatest chance of success.

COLLABORATIVE ADVANTAGE CHECKLIST: PREPARING TO COLLABORATE

- ■ Have you established a process for assessing collaborative opportunities, as part of your strategic planning processes?
- ■ Do you keep track of potential, previous, or existing partners as part of your intelligence-gathering processes?
- ■ Do you participate in a range of networks and associations that will enable you to meet potential partners?
- ■ Do you have a set of agreed criteria for assessing potential partners, with which the relevant people in the organization are familiar?
- ■ Have you built in the necessary time to explore different options for collaboration with potential partners?
- ■ Have you considered using a low-risk "test and learn" project to determine whether a particular partnership will be effective?
- ■ Have you discussed an exit strategy as part of the planning discussions with specific partners?
- ■ Do you have a means of identifying the individual(s) who have the right capability profile to represent your organization in a potential collaboration?

3 Structuring

The structure of a collaborative venture needs careful consideration, as the right structure will support and enable effective working, and the wrong structure will get in the way. There are four main structuring issues to consider. These are:

▶ Choosing an overall organizational form. There are many options to choose from, ranging from informal relationships, through various framework agreements, to creating an independent legal entity.
▶ Structuring the day-to-day governance of the collaboration, in terms of decision-making processes and accountabilities.
▶ The model for allocating costs and benefits to the different partners.
▶ The policy on intellectual property, covering both existing intellectual property and dealing with any new intellectual property arising from the venture.

Bear in mind that initial decisions may well be revised as the collaboration develops and circumstances evolve, but an agreed and clearly communicated governance structure is essential to get the collaboration off to a good start.

Choosing a legal form

Collaborative ventures take many different forms, and their legal status varies widely, depending on the particular aims of the group and the options available to them in their particular geography. It would not be possible to give a description of every option here but we can suggest some of the key questions to help you make an informed choice.

QUESTIONS TO HELP LEGAL STRUCTURING

▶ Who are the partners who will share responsibility for achieving joint outcomes?

▶ Who are key stakeholders who need to be involved but not necessarily as part of the formal governance structure of the venture?

▶ What type of decision-making process best suits the aims of the collaboration and the number of partners involved?

▶ What are the pros and cons of setting up a separate legal entity? For example, is it important to have a vehicle for hiring employees, bringing in funds, owning intellectual property?

▶ What is the expected timescale of this collaboration, and how might that influence the choice of legal structure? (for example, people may not want to join an independent entity as employees if it has a limited lifespan)

▶ Have you considered the full range of possibilities—for example, an informal arrangement, formal framework agreement, company, partnership, charitable foundation?

▶ If new intellectual property is created, where will ownership of that be held?

▶ What legal forms have other similar collaborative ventures used? Which seem to have been most successful?

The discussions about legal form may take place during the preparation phase for a collaboration, and the individuals who are then directly involved in the collaboration on a day-to-day basis may simply inherit that decision. Equally, it is possible that no specific legal structure is agreed during the strategic decision-making phase, and the partners will need to work out the best option together during the goal alignment phase. As ever, form should follow function. The best structure for a collaborative venture will entirely depend on the particular circumstances, aims, and membership of that consortium of member organizations. It is important that the people involved in the process think laterally and creatively about the options, by investigating the possibilities within their country's legal framework. It is best to seek legal advice on the options available and the costs and benefits of each.

The boxes give examples of two different legal structures, to illustrate some of the issues involved.

THE STORY OF MAXXIUM

Joint venture Maxxium was set up in 1999 as a new legal entity, by Rémy Cointreau opening its global distribution network outside the United States to other shareholders—initially two other companies, Edrington and Jim Beam Brands. Despite Rémy Cointreau having a significantly higher turnover than the two other shareholders, a conscious decision was made for the new company to have equal shareholdings from the three partners. When a fourth shareholder, Swedish firm V&S, owner of the Absolut Vodka brand, joined several years later, the same philosophy was applied and the shareholdings of all four were balanced out at 25 percent. Maxxium believes that this creates the right spirit of egalitarianism, and it applies the same principle of equal shareholdings when Maxxium itself enters into joint ventures in particular geographical markets.

As demonstrated by Maxxium, legal structure needs to reflect the philosophy of the venture as well as what makes the most commercial sense.

THE STORY OF GROUPE DANONE AND YAKULT HONSHA

Paris-based Groupe Danone and Tokyo-based Yakult Honsha formed a strategic alliance in 2004 to strengthen their global leadership in probiotics and accelerate the growth of both companies. The structuring of the alliance had a number of different components:

▶ Groupe Danone nominated two individuals to Yakult Honsha's Board of Directors while Yakult nominated one individual to Danone's Board of Directors.
▶ The two companies jointly established a Liaison Office to identify specific areas of collaboration, starting with the area of probiotics outside of Japan, and also to be responsible for the facilitation of joint projects such as entry into new markets, joint research and development and other business projects identified over time.
▶ The two companies also decided to create a Global Probiotics Council to act as an influencing body to advance the cause of probiotics with relevant stakeholders such as consumers, regulatory authorities, and the scientific community.

Groupe Danone was already the largest shareholder of Yakult Honsha with a 20 percent stake. Cross-shareholdings is another possible choice that can be made in terms of structuring a relationship, with the obvious additional motivation that it creates to find a win for both parties.

Contractual agreements

The other consideration in terms of legal form is of course the contractual structure for any specific activity undertaken by the collaborative venture. Again, it is not possible to cover the range of possibilities in detail here, but the broader learning point emerging from companies with a great deal of collaboration experience is that many forms of collaboration benefit from having a light framework agreement rather than iron-clad contracts.

As David Hawkins, Operations Director of PSL, a UK-based advisor on building business relationships, says:

> *Contracts are written to cover failure, not success. I was involved in long contractual negotiations between my previous company and a Chinese company. After months of work the lengthy contract was presented to the managing director of the Chinese firm. After casting his eye over it briefly he shook his head and said "Too many words. We make, you pay, everybody's happy." And on that basis the deal was done.*

PSL encourages organizations to develop partnering agreements that spell out the measurable objectives of the partnership but leave a great deal of freedom and flexibility as to the "how" of achieving it. In addition, they recommend the development of partnering charters to cover agreed ways of working and softer issues that can be appended to the partnering agreement. Although lawyers may be uncomfortable with this style of contract, it provides a clear framework of both outcomes and shared principles, and is thus designed for achieving success rather than focusing on the penalties for failure.

David Hawkins further illustrates the point with an example from everyday life:

> *I contracted with a local plumber to put a new bathroom in my house. He brought in the tiler, the plasterer, the electrician, all independent contractors in their own right but who regularly worked together on projects. As they did a good job my neighbour decided to get them in as well, but as he knew the electrician he contracted through him. The same team came together and delivered another good result.*

What held this small, flexible partnership together was not a contract—
or even one particular way of contracting with customers—but a
realization that if any one of them let the others down, they would lose
a significant stream of business. The prospect of future work together—
what cooperation expert Robert Axelrod called "the shadow of the
future"[1]—was the binding force, not a legal straitjacket.

Governance structures

We cannot cover every possible approach to governance of a collaborative
venture, as the only limit is one's imagination, but it may be interesting to
reflect on one or two real-life examples to give a sense of the decision-
making process involved. The first is an example from the high-tech sector
in the United Kingdom, involving a partnership to deliver one of the
biggest information technology contracts ever awarded, the second from
the higher education sector in the United States.

THE STORY OF THE ASPIRE PROGRAM

**Fujitsu Services, part of the family of companies owned by global technology
giant Fujitsu, provides IT infrastructure management and outsourcing services
to customers across Europe, the Middle East, and Africa. The company's website highlights its ability to collaborate, as a selling point for the company:**

> *We operate through a wide range of relationships with our customers, from full out-
> sourcing through managed services, professional services and projects. We
> recognize the value to customers of alliances and partnering arrangements, and
> are experienced in acting as prime integrator, alliance partner and sub-contractor.*[2]

**One of Fujitsu's largest customer projects in recent years is a collaboration with
consulting firm Capgemini to deliver technology services to the UK's tax
authority, the Inland Revenue. Known as the ASPIRE program (Acquiring
Strategic Partners for the Inland rEvenue), the £3 billion-plus contract was
awarded in December 2003 to a consortium led by Capgemini, with Fujitsu
Services and British Telecom as key partners. The Inland Revenue included an
assessment of whether consortium members would work well together as one
of its selection criteria. Fujitsu Services and Capgemini had worked in partnership on a range of projects going back more than 20 years, and therefore had
the advantage of established relationships right up to board level. Interestingly,
Capgemini, like Fujitsu, promotes its ability to collaborate as a marketing message for the firm. Capgemini's home page highlights the following quote from
its chief executive Paul Hermelin:**

Collaboration is not something you can teach employees in a day course, it's part of a company's culture and DNA. I believe Capgemini fits the bill perfectly.[3]

Tim Gibson, director for EMEA at Fujitsu Services, described some of the factors that he believes have contributed to the success of the partnership with Capgemini. First of all, he underlines the importance of a very clear work share. Knowing who is doing what—and for the customer to understand that as well—is essential. Fujitsu Services and Capgemini assessed their respective capabilities, where they had underlaps or overlaps, then allocated very clear responsibilities in terms of the delivery of this particular project. They chose not to set up a separate joint venture company—partially because of the difficulty of attracting employees to an organization whose longevity would be determined by the longevity of the client project—but rather, determined which company's employees had the right skills to undertake particular tasks. Capgemini was the prime contractor, with Fujitsu as sub-contractor, but the relationship is described by both as a true partnership.

In addition to the primary partners in this particular consortium, there are several tiers of sub-contractors with different levels of involvement. These relationships are also managed carefully by Capgemini and Fujitsu, but it was clear from the outset that these other firms would not be involved in the management of the contract and the direct relationship with the client. Both Capgemini and Fujitsu refer to the overall collaborative structure as an "ecosystem," and believe that the approach they have selected puts the best skills on the right tasks, while maintaining a very clear accountability structure for the client.

Second, the governance process needed to be clear and effective. A joint Capgemini–Fujitsu board-level meeting is held every four weeks to ensure any strategic or operational matters are dealt with in good time. This is in addition to the formal project board structure which was set up by the Inland Revenue, has representation from the Inland Revenue, Capgemini and Fujitsu, and also has regular meetings. Alongside this top-level governance process, three major decision-making bodies were set up as part of the collaborative structure, with nominated individuals heading each of these: one for the overall technology architecture, one on commercial issues, and one to handle day-to-day operational issues. These three bodies know that they can escalate issues to the monthly board-level meeting as required, for rapid resolution.

Third, it is important to note that the two principal partners (Capgemini and Fujitsu) are also competitors in other spheres. To create a climate of trust, several factors come into play. One is the importance of good personal relationships between individuals on the team, built up over time. Tim Gibson points out that once established, these relationships enable the two organizations to take on other joint projects much more quickly and easily, and they therefore actively seek opportunities to do so. Another pragmatic step is to ensure that everyone involved signs non-disclosure agreements to ensure that commercially confidential information shared by one organization is not used inappropriately or shared more widely by the other. The desire to maintain a long-term profitable commercial relationship is the greatest motivator to respecting confidentiality, but the legal documents act as a reminder of the importance of this. Gibson points out the importance of absolute transparency in dealing with a particular partner, such as openly discussing whether to compete or partner on a particular bid, keeping the best outcome for both firms—and the client—firmly in mind.

THE STORY OF FIVE COLLEGES INC.

In the Pioneer Valley in western Massachusetts, a consortium of colleges has operated in collaboration with one another since the 1950s. Initially an informal collaboration between three liberal arts colleges—Amherst, Mount Holyoke, and Smith—and the Amherst campus of the state university (University of Massachusetts), the consortium grew to include a fourth liberal arts college which was established in 1970, Hampshire College. This fourth college was in fact a product of the collaboration between the other institutions: they jointly decided to found an innovative liberal arts college which would implement many of the ideas from a joint review the presidents of the other four schools had completed on the future of liberal arts education.

A non-profit institution called Five Colleges Inc. was set up in 1965 to coordinate and support the collaborative working between the five institutions, including the founding of Hampshire College, which opened its doors in 1970.

The collaboration has continued to thrive and focuses on:

▶ shared use of educational and cultural resources and facilities such as libraries and museums
▶ joint departments and programs
▶ joint facilities such as the inter-campus transportation system and a fiber optic network.

The Five Colleges Inc. staff of 16, headed by executive director Lorna Peterson, has established a governance structure centered around three main Five College committees:

▶ The Board of Directors, which includes the presidents of the five member institutions and which makes the major strategic and operational decisions. It meets monthly.

▶ **The Deans Council, made up of the deans of faculty from the five institutions, which meets twice a month and has a summer retreat. This council focuses primarily on academic collaboration issues such as curriculum development and joint faculty appointments.**

▶ **The Principal Business Officers—the group of chief financial officers from the five-member institutions, who meet once a month. This group focuses primarily on general funding issues and administrative collaboration.**

In addition to these governance committees, there are approximately 70 other Five College committees in place to facilitate interworking. Half of these are faculty groups and half are administrative staff from the five institutions, as collaboration is encouraged and supported in both the academic and administrative domains.

Lorna Peterson says: "Our committee structure ensures that all constituencies know each other across the five institutions. From communication comes trust. You have to get people together—otherwise you cannot create a culture of co-operation." Lorna or a member of her staff attends every Five College committee meeting, and is on hand to give help and advice on, for example, getting funding for particular initiatives, or gaining support from the Deans Council or Board of Directors for new ideas.

The stories of the Aspire program and Five Colleges Inc. illustrate the need to establish a governance structure which facilitates effective decision-making across the different partners. Depending on the legal form you have selected, you may have certain governance structures imposed upon you, such as the need to set up a board with non-executive members. If you are establishing an independent entity to manage the collaborative process, you may need to write job descriptions and hire appropriate employees for the new structure. All of these processes take time and as suggested above, a cost–benefit analysis is necessary to determine whether they are worthwhile.

Regardless of the legal form chosen, things then have to get done. Decisions have to be made, information needs to be shared, different stakeholders have to be managed. Most collaborative ventures find that it is necessary to look at governance at two levels, the strategic and the operational. Typically the main partners are part of a strategic decision-making body—which may be called a board, a steering group, a lead body, or a management committee—that handles major decisions about overall direction, structure and resourcing of the collaboration, as well as responding to issues raised to it from the operational level. This strategic body also acts as a mediator when any issues arise between partners at the operational level. It is the body that must remain focused on the overall aims of the collaboration and the charter agreed at the start, and it is accountable for achieving the agreed goals of the collaborative venture. Therefore continuity of membership is important, as is real commitment to the collaborative process.

Bearing in mind that collaborative ventures are likely to have a number of work streams to oversee, there will probably be a requirement for more than one operational work group. These may be called work groups, executive boards, task forces, or project teams—as ever, there is no standard terminology. The process linking the operational work to the strategic decision making will need to be mapped out and communicated.

As we have said before, there is no one way to structure the operational tasks of these groups, but the questions in the box may help ensure that you do not miss any key points.

QUESTIONS TO HELP ESTABLISH GOVERNANCE STRUCTURES

Strategic level

▶ Have you conformed with any specific governance requirements dictated by the legal form you have selected?
▶ Is every major partner represented?
▶ Which decisions must be put before this group, and what is the process for doing so?
▶ What is the process for raising operational issues to this group?

Operational level

▶ Which aspects of the collaborative venture's activities warrant a working team?
▶ For each of those work areas, which partners should be represented and who is best to represent them?
▶ What support resources do the working groups need, if any (for example, project management or administrative resource)?
▶ How will these teams interact with each other and with the strategic decision-making body?

Generic issues to consider for both strategic and operational levels

▶ Which individuals will represent the partner organizations on these groups?
▶ Do the individuals have the right skills, level of commitment, and time available to fulfill their role?
▶ Do the individuals have the right seniority and level of influence to keep their organization committed to the collaborative process or resolve issues?

▶ Are the relevant meeting dates set well in advance in everyone's diaries?
▶ Is there appropriate administrative support for the group?
▶ How will the group members communicate with each other between meetings?
▶ Will there be an appointed or a rotating chair for the group?
▶ Will an external facilitator be used for some or all of the meetings?
▶ How will decisions from the group be documented and communicated?

Allocating costs and benefits

The Five Colleges story has another interesting facet, in that the five institutions involved share the staff costs of Five Colleges Inc. equally, despite different student numbers and budget sizes. Lorna Peterson credits the founding fathers of the consortium with the foresight to realize that the principle of equal shares helps to generate a sense of trust and teamwork. For other shared costs, different formulae were developed. For example, for the shared library management system, a system based on elevenths rather than fifths was developed, and works well. For sharing the costs of the fiber optics network a systems based on sevenths was agreed. For the shared museums database, an allocation of costs based on twelfths was put in place. The precision of these algorithms demonstrates the care and attention that was put into developing the right allocation for each particular process.

A further sharing of costs is evident in the fact that every campus hosts at least one Five College academic program, and as part of that pays for the necessary office space for the faculty members and administrative staff involved, even though their salary costs are shared with the other institutions. Lorna Peterson says:

> *Collaboration is such an enriching experience for the faculty and staff members involved that we decided not to split hairs on costs. As long as the balance is perceived to be fair and we give regular feedback on what the member institutions are getting for their money, then it works.*

There can be no single algorithm to allocate costs and benefits fairly across a collaborative venture. The important step is to discuss the different costs and benefits and the relative contribution of each partner, in both tangible (for example, money or staff) and intangible (for example, influence or reputation) terms. The challenge is to then apply creativity, imagination, and a sense of fair play to the allocation process, ensuring that all partners are satisfied with the end result. Whichever formulae are agreed, they should be kept under regular review as circumstances and relative contributions may change.

Handling intellectual property

Intellectual property rights can be a thorny issue in collaborative ventures. Intellectual property (IP) is defined as:

Content of the human intellect deemed to be unique and original and to have marketplace value—and thus to warrant protection under the law. Intellectual property includes but is not limited to ideas; inventions; literary works; chemical, business, or computer processes; and company or product names and logos. Intellectual property protections fall into four categories: copyright (for literary works, art, and music), trademarks (for company and product names and logos), patents (for inventions and processes), and trade secrets (for recipes, code, and processes).[4]

Especially in collaborative ventures involving competitors, it can be difficult to reconcile the need to respect commercial confidentiality with the need for openness. Two aspects are relevant: the approach to sharing existing intellectual property, and the approach to dealing with intellectual property that arises as a result of the collaboration.

In terms of sharing existing intellectual property, it is often useful to ask each partner to sign a non-disclosure agreement (NDA) relating to intellectual property shared amongst the partners involved in the collaboration. This generally commits each partner not to share the IP concerned beyond the confines of the collaborative venture. Although signing such an agreement does not guarantee that IP will not leak out, it does give the IP owner a means of redress if confidentiality is breached. The act of signing the NDA is a signal to all concerned that this is an expected behavior norm for the partners. It may be a point worth covering in any collaboration charter that is developed, a process that will be covered in the next chapter. Nonetheless, no matter how many legal documents are signed, it is ultimately a question of judgment whether particular information is shared within a collaborative group. The people representing their organizations need to be able to judge whether the risk of the sharing the information is balanced or outweighed by a potential benefit.

In terms of intellectual property generated by the collaboration, the approach to ownership and use of that IP should be determined at the outset, in this structuring phase. This can be a more complicated issue when the collaboration does not have a separate legal identity, and the development of significant intellectual property is often one of the motivations to set up a legal entity.

In any case, there can be a real or imagined threat of partners "stealing" intellectual property. By discussing this issue openly in the early stages of a collaboration, future conflicts may be minimized or avoided altogether. The questions in the box may provide a useful framework.

QUESTIONS TO HELP DEAL WITH INTELLECTUAL PROPERTY ISSUES

▶ How will existing intellectual property belonging to partner organizations be handled? What are the rights and responsibilities of the other partners?

▶ How will new intellectual property, created by the venture, be handled? Where will ownership lie, and what rights and responsibilities will the different partners have?

▶ What are the rights and responsibilities of the partners with regard to each other's confidential information, whether or not it technically qualifies as "intellectual property"?

Assigning accountabilities

Many of the roles and responsibilities that need to be established within a collaborative venture are the same as would be established for any work project. However there are some specific considerations for roles within a collaborative venture that it is not normally necessary to consider when establishing roles within the boundaries of one organization. These distinctions are worth highlighting here.

THE BALANCE OF POWER

The need to keep an equitable balance of power across the different partners means that choices such as the person to chair the strategic decision-making body are not simply a case of picking the best individual for the role. Whoever is given such a role will inevitably be perceived as having more power than others in the group. Therefore a collaborative venture should consider a range of more democratic options such as:

▶ a rotating chair
▶ joint chairmen
▶ an elected chair
▶ having meetings facilitated with no specific chair appointed
▶ a non-executive chair from outside the partnership group.

DEDICATED RESOURCES

More will be said about resourcing collaborative work in Chapter 6. The point here is that one of the major pitfalls in collaborative working is the danger of underestimating the resources needed to achieve something. A significant number of collaborative efforts report a phenomenon of collective delusion, where the partner organizations, at least for a time, assume that all of the work can be done by people contributing part-time to a collaborative effort, on top of busy "day jobs." This is rarely possible, and at some point the realization dawns that some dedicated resource will be required. Project management is often the key capability needed. There is often an assumption that because a collaborative effort has a number of partners, their collective energy and goodwill will be enough to make things happen. Be aware that collaborative work needs the same pragmatic doers assigned to it that any work does—and dedicated resource is often even more important in view of the additional coordination and communication work required in a collaborative setting.

GATEKEEPERS

For many collaborative ventures, especially those focused on developing or delivering products and services, the partners are likely to have multiple contacts between people in different parts of their organizations. As long as everyone involved is included in the communication processes of the venture, this is a perfectly workable model. However, certain key decisions, relationships, and/or communication processes may need to be managed in a coordinated fashion, and it is at times important to assign gatekeeping roles to particular individuals. For example, it may be that only one representative of a partner organization should "officially" brief the other stakeholders within his or her organization on matters to do with the collaborative venture, to avoid confusing messages being disseminated. Or perhaps all operational issues from a particular partner need to be channeled through one individual so that one person has the overview of the current issues. Another example might be that one person is identified as the relationship manager with a sub-contractor, and a clear request is made to the other partners to copy all matters relating to that sub-contractor to that person. The gatekeeper role is simply a way of ensuring that where coordination is required, there is a named individual taking responsibility for it. Creating an unnecessary level of bureaucracy or duplication of effort is not the aim. The lesson from many collaborative ventures is that coordination is a set of accountabilities, not simply a stated wish.

Gatekeeping roles often exist in two spheres: gatekeepers managing relationships with each partner organization, and gatekeepers representing the collaborative body as a whole, perhaps on a particular issue or with a particular stakeholder. For example, in the drinks-brand-building distribution partnership Maxxium, whose story was told earlier, gatekeeper roles were created giving particular partners responsibility for specific categories of drink (such as whisky or vodka). These individuals could then allow or veto the entry of competing brands into the Maxxium distribution network, depending on the market conditions. This gave the shareholder companies clear control over an area that might otherwise have led to significant conflict of interest.

Flexible structures

Whatever decisions you make about structure for a particular collaborative venture, there will inevitably be changes in circumstances over the lifetime of the venture that will require changes to the initial structure. New projects will mean new working groups; a change in legislation may prompt a change of legal form; the addition of a new partner might mean a different approach to decision-making. An effective collaboration learns and adapts, senses and responds. Flexibility is essential.

COLLABORATIVE ADVANTAGE CHECKLIST: STRUCTURING THE
COLLABORATIVE PROCESS

- Have you obtained legal advice on the different organizational forms available to you, and their respective costs and benefits?
- Have you investigated the structures used by other similar collaborative ventures?
- Have you developed a governance structure for decision-making at both the strategic and operational levels?
- Have you ensured that an equitable balance of power is in place—in terms of both reality and perception?
- Have you considered how relationships with other stakeholders (for example, sub-contractors) will be managed from within the collaborating group?
- Have you assigned key roles to specific individuals and communicated this as appropriate?
- Have you determined which gatekeeping roles are required—for the collaboration as a whole and for each partner organization?
- Are there any dedicated roles that need to be put in place at the outset to support the collaborative venture—for example, management, administrative, or project management roles?
- Have you developed a model for how costs and benefits will be allocated, and agreed this with all partners concerned?
- Have you agreed an approach to dealing with intellectual property, both existing and new?

4 Integrating the Team and Agreeing Joint Outcomes

If the preparation and structuring phases have been handled well, you should find yourself with a group of partners committed to embarking on a collaborative endeavor, with a reasonable understanding of the outcomes being sought and the different wins for each party. By now you will have agreed a top-level structure, and you will have identified the individuals who will play the key roles at a strategic and an operational level.

Then the first crucial planning meeting will take place. It is crucial because:

▶ The first meeting establishes the shared understanding of what this group is aiming to achieve.
▶ It is the first time that this particular collaborative venture begins to build an identity as a distinct process.
▶ It is likely to be the first time that a particular group of individuals has met, and it is when all-important first impressions are formed.
▶ The style of the first meeting sets the tone for all subsequent meetings.

This first formal meeting of the different partners is where the real alignment process begins. The people around the table come from different organizations. They have different expectations, different working processes, different experiences of collaborative working, different aims, different concerns, different personal ambitions. Even if the preparation phase has scoped the aim of the collaborative venture from a strategic and organizational perspective, it will not have achieved alignment for every individual involved in the process. This process of building a shared understanding across a number of people—not just a number of organizations—begins when they first have the opportunity to meet. In this chapter we move from strategic considerations to look at some of the nitty-gritty, practical steps that are especially important in the first few meetings of a collaborative group.

Knowing what to aim for

Regardless of the type of collaborative venture, whether small or large in scope, there are some common aims for the early meetings of any collaborative group. Expressed as outcomes, these are as follows:

▶ The desired outcomes for the collaborative venture are agreed and circulated in writing to all partners for comment.
▶ Each partner feels valued and that his or her views have been heard.
▶ Initial roles and responsibilities are clear to all concerned—while recognizing that these may change as the collaborative venture evolves.
▶ The key stakeholders for this venture are identified, and a plan developed to enable the collaborative venture to manage those stakeholder relationships.

It is probably a fair assumption that at the first meeting, there will be little real trust between the individuals involved, unless this is a group that has worked together before. Therefore it is the first opportunity to build some trust. Many people will arrive at a meeting like this with their "hidden agenda" radar switched firmly on, looking for power games or Machiavellian plots that may or not be there. This is one reason that some organizations with experience of collaborative working bring in an independent process facilitator from outside the collaborative group to facilitate the first meeting—and sometimes subsequent meetings too, especially when some conflict resolution is required. This independent person, with no political agenda or affiliation to a particular partner, can take responsibility for the meeting process, enabling the partners to participate fully.

THE STORY OF AN EFFICIENT CONSUMER RESPONSE (ECR) INITIATIVE

The retail industry has increasingly begun to emulate pioneers such as Wal-Mart by working in closer partnership with the vendors that supply them with goods. A process sometimes referred to as Efficient Consumer Response (ECR) brings retailers together with their key vendors to look at developing more efficient replenishment, assortment, product introduction, and promotion processes in particular product categories. The significant shift that has occurred in recent years is that retailers are inviting selected vendors to help them manage the relevant product category in their stores—leading to the interesting challenge of suppliers advising on their competitors' products as well as their own.

Blueprint Management Consultants, a Scotland-based consultancy that specializes in the fast-moving consumer goods (FMCG) sector, were asked to facilitate a significant ECR exercise between a major retailer and 25 of its leading vendors. Each vendor represented a particular category of product, and was invited to work collaboratively with the retailer to improve that product category. The process that Blueprint helped to design and facilitate involved approximately seven one-day workshops over a three-month period for each category, with about a dozen executives from both the retailer and a vendor at each event. As there were 25 such work streams, this was an enormous commitment of time and resources from the retailer, which participated in each stream.

Ronnie Macdonald, founder and managing director of Blueprint, explained why it was important to have an independent facilitator managing the process:

> There were a number of benefits to having us involved. First of all, we were the honest broker. If the retailer started using these events to negotiate better margins for themselves, which has been the traditional approach to working with suppliers, we hit that with a big stick. If the suppliers started focusing on branding issues, we hit that with a big stick too, reminding both sides that these events were about category management. We also helped the two teams through the inevitable sticky moments where it was hard to find the win–win for both sides on specific issues.

In this particular example the facilitation costs were paid for by the vendors, even though the initiative came from the retailer. The vendors that participated felt this was a worthwhile investment for the opportunity to be the lead company helping to manage a whole category of products for a major customer. According to Ronnie Macdonald, some of the most worthwhile retailer–supplier partnerships of this kind develop from a vendor successfully focusing on the overall growth and success of a category, and if necessary sacrificing short-term wins for their own products.

Establishing personal relationships and trust

To set the right tone and give personal relationships the chance to be established, the early part of the meeting should enable people to get to know each other. Every individual should be heard. If possible, you should consider a residential event, especially for the first meeting. This gives the group an opportunity to socialize as well as work together, an essential ingredient in the trust-building process. As most people will know from experience, the time spent discussing issues informally in a bar or restaurant often produces the most valuable conversations of all—and the sharing of information about families, hobbies, likes and dislikes turns a collaboration partner into a real human being. If you are able to hold the first meeting as a residential event, it is often useful to start with dinner one evening, keep formal input to a minimum, and simply give people an opportunity to get to know each other. By the time you start the formal discussions the following morning, you will have a group of people who know something about each other and are ready to move into productive discussions. As you have them all in situ, you will have also avoided the frequent problem of people arriving late because of travel difficulties and missing the introductions at the start of the meeting.

There are many things that can make a big difference when a collaborative group first meets. With experience, you will become sensitized to the small things that can have major consequences. Here are a few of the most common pitfalls that are easily avoided once you are aware of them.

PEOPLE ARRIVING LATE OR LEAVING EARLY

People who arrive late for the first meeting—whatever the reason may be, and even if it is only by a quarter of an hour—will be seen by the other partners as less committed to the process. That first negative impression will be set, and may take some time to be readjusted. Leaving early will have the same effect. Therefore checking that everyone can be there for the whole event is an important part of managing the process.

SETTING THE AGENDA

People who treat the first collaborative meeting like any other meeting may make the mistake of applying a traditional meeting structure to it. In other words, someone determines the agenda, fills every minute of the meeting with agenda items, and perhaps even structures it around presentations, leaving little time for discussion. This may result in some information being shared, but it will not result in the outcomes set for this first collaborative meeting: building trust and aligning goals.

A different approach is needed. First, any formal agenda, if one is required, should be proposed and discussed with all the partners before being set. Second, the first meeting needs a lot of open space for discussion. The social time will give some of that, but the meeting structure should also allow for open discussion. It is unlikely that the first meeting will be any shorter than a full day, and in view of the earlier comments about social time, at least a day and a half is preferable.

PEOPLE DELEGATING ATTENDANCE

A key design principle that needs to be covered in the structuring phase is whether it is acceptable for people to delegate attendance at the meetings of a collaborative group. Even if it is decided that it is acceptable to do so in certain circumstances, it is essential that at the first meeting the key players are there. If some key people cannot make a date, pick a date that they can make. Trust is built between individuals, not organizations.

PHYSICAL WORKING ENVIRONMENT

The physical working environment can make a huge difference to how a group feels about working together. If you want a collaborative venture to get off to a bad start, book your first meeting in a cramped airless room with no windows, and provide standard sandwiches as the lunchtime fare. If you want to increase its chances of success, book a nice hotel or conference centre away from any of the partners' offices, provide a light airy room with lots of space and natural light, and make sure the catering is good. This does not necessarily mean spending lots of money—voluntary organizations that have to watch their spending are very skilled at finding comfortable venues that are good value for money. However it is a false economy to skimp on the budget for meetings and put people into an environment that they cannot wait to escape. A pleasant working environment is one way to say that this venture is important, and that the people who are participating are valued.

SEATING PLAN

Linked to the physical working environment is the question of how people are seated in the room. Of course this will depend on the numbers involved, but the key design principle should be openness and equality of status. Round tables are always effective, or even people seated in a semi-circle or circle without any tables at all. Having no physical barriers contributes to relationship building, although sometimes it is simply not a practical option. If there are presentations from the front, ensure everyone can see equally well, and that everyone is close enough to engage in a dialogue.

 If people are sat around one table, be conscious of any seat or seat that traditionally denotes more power—for example a seat at the head of a long table—and avoid having anyone in that particular position.

INTRODUCTIONS

If it is possible for participants to have some social time together before the formal start of the meeting, the personal introductions can be handled informally at that point. However it is a good idea, even if people have been introduced, to give everyone a chance to speak at the start of formal proceedings. If this is the point at which introductions are made, something as simple as asking people to say something about their interests outside work can completely shift the tone of the meeting. Again, the purpose is to get people to come out from behind their organizational façade and appear as human beings. You might initially be a bit wary of the finance director from PartnerCo, but once you see him as Jim who climbed Mount Everest last year and whose wife has just had triplets, a whole different perspective will open up.

Once introductions have been made, you will need a further icebreaker to warm up the group. One useful exercise is to ask participants what their hopes and fears are regarding the collaborative venture. This gives them permission to open up and talk about their feelings rather than keeping them hidden. It values and recognizes every individual in the room, and it provides a good list of things to try to foster (or avoid) throughout the collaborative process.

Many managers are very task-focused. Investing time and energy in building a foundation of personal relationships and trust can be a new experience for many people. It may feel like time-wasting when in fact it is one of the most essential aspects of building collaborative advantage. It is simple: if you build trust, effective collaboration will follow. If you do not, it will not. Therefore knowing how to shape the group's working process in order to develop trust is a key skill.

If trust building does not come naturally to the participants in the collaborative venture, bring in an external person who has that capability, to facilitate the group's interactions. The first few meetings are especially important in this regard. Once trust and good working relationships are established, the group will be better able to focus on the task in hand, and there will be less of a need to craft its working process. However, as we discuss in Chapter 5, a collaborative venture must always keep a watchful eye on the way people are working together. There can be conflicts or breakdowns in communication at any time, and these need to be handled before they cause irreparable damage to the collaborative process.

Aligning goals

The process of aligning the different partners to a common goal or set of goals is particularly challenging in a collaborative setting. It is difficult enough to achieve within the boundaries of one organization where, at least in theory, people share common aims. Therefore the first meetings of a collaborative group need to build that consensus. There will of course already have been discussions on common goals in the preparation and structuring phases. However, it is likely that people who were not involved in those conversations will be at the first planning meeting. Therefore, it is extremely unwise to assume that there is a common understanding of what this collaborative venture is trying to achieve. In many post-project reviews and lessons learnt exercises, people realize that things went wrong because they had a different understanding of what was meant to happen in the first place. For a collaborative venture, real effort has to be invested very early on, in order to avoid this particular pitfall.

The process of developing consensus on a common goal cannot be rushed. You might like to consider working through the three steps outlined in the box.

A process for agreeing common goals

1. Ask the group to brainstorm the criteria that they believe should be fulfilled by any joint goal. Examples of criteria this could include are:
    a Agreed by all parties.
    b Measurable.
    c Achievable within six months.
    d Must be managed using existing resources.
    This discussion has the added advantage of helping people understand each other's perspectives better.
2. Share the "official" goal of the collaborative venture as determined in the preparation and structuring phase, if there is one already agreed. This brings everyone up to the same point of understanding, whether they were part of developing the original goal or not. Give everyone the opportunity to ask questions or share concerns about the agreed goal. Check the goal against the criteria previously identified. Modify as required.
3. Even if an overarching aim has already been agreed, this is rarely expressed as a SMART (specific, measurable, agreed, realistic, time-related) objective. Spend further time as needed working the overall objectives through to something specific and clear. When the shared goal (or goals) has been agreed, make sure it is documented, as this will serve as the baseline for the work to follow.

You may choose to define some early wins on the way to a longer-term goal. The main tests that you need to apply to the agreed goals are:

▶ Do these objectives meet the main strategic criteria for this collaborative venture?
▶ Are these objectives committed to by every one of the partners?
▶ Are these expressed in a way that can be communicated to the partners and other stakeholders?

Visualizing success

A collaborative effort is usually sustained by the enthusiasm and commitment of the people involved. The strategic commitment of their organizations is always necessary but never sufficient to carry the group through the ups and downs of collaborative endeavors. In shaping the initial goals, you may wish to consider connecting with the hearts as well as the brains of the people involved. One way of doing this is to use creative, visual means to express the aims of the group. As they say, a picture is worth a thousand words.

A VISUALIZATION EXERCISE

Once you have some shared understanding of the overall aims of the venture, a useful exercise is to ask the group members—working individually, in pairs or in trios depending on numbers—to create a visual image of what the success of this collaboration would look like for them, looking forward one or two years. There are many options for the materials you could use, from paints to collage materials. Armed with enough flipchart paper, Blu-tack and creative materials (scissors, glue, a stack of magazines, and marker pens are a good starting point and not too messy), each individual (or small team) then creates a picture of success as they see it. Because so much of organizational life revolves around the written word, people should be encouraged to use images rather than words. Providing materials such as magazines for images helps reduce the anxiety of people who feel they have no artistic ability. Once each individual or team has produced a work of art, these can be displayed around the walls of the room, and each individual or team then explains the picture to the rest of the group. A whole new range of insights will result from this exercise, and it has the added advantage of being energizing and fun.

It is important to be aware, however, that many people have been conditioned to believe that fun is not an acceptable part of organizational life. Also, senior people may feel that the somewhat playful process described in the box does not sit well with their status. However, this is precisely why the exercise can be so valuable. Participating in an exercise such as this means that people step out from behind their organizational façade, tap in to their creative and playful side, and open up in a way that they may not be used to doing. Again, a skilled facilitator can create a climate in which people feel creatively challenged rather than threatened, and you will soon find the room filled with a lot of laughter and interaction as the pictures reveal aspects that would never have emerged in the more traditional, left-brained approach to discussing goals.

Agreeing ways of working: a collaboration charter

Another important part of the early alignment phase is the process of agreeing some norms and values for the group. In other words, it is not just objectives that are important but the way in which they are reached. It is useful to discuss ways of working explicitly in the first meeting. The discussion itself will bring to light different individual, cultural, or organizational perspectives, and will surface the mental models of the participants with regard to collaboration.

One useful way of eliciting people's thoughts on this is to ask them to reflect on their previous experiences of collaborative working. Ask them to identify specific examples of effective and ineffective collaboration from their own experience, then share the factors that made these experiences positive or negative. An example of the output from this type of discussion is given in the box.

What works	What doesn't work
Common purpose	Hidden agendas
Everyone contributing	Some partners not committed
Recognizing everyone's contribution	One partner taking all the credit
Enough resources available	Expecting everyone to do this part-time
Action oriented	A "talk shop"
Clear roles	Unclear accountabilities

It is useful for people to illustrate their points by giving specific examples of the experiences they have had. The stories bring the points to life and avoid the conversation remaining theoretical. This discussion will add to the knowledge that people will have about each other, and contribute to the relationship-building process.

By creating a collaboration charter together, the participants will articulate what they believe are important principles to live by for the life of this particular collaborative effort. You may wish to express them as principles or alternatively as a set of rights and responsibilities. As with the agreed goals, these principles should be documented and shared with all participants after the first meeting. Some collaborative groups have written up their charter and asked each participant to sign it—not as a legal obligation but as a demonstration of commitment to the process. This charter, signed by all, becomes a symbol of the commitments made, and although many things may change and evolve as the collaborative working progresses, it can act as something of a touchstone for the group when it loses its way or if breakdowns occur. It can also be very useful for communication purposes to other stakeholders. An example is given in the box.

THE STORY OF THE GLOBAL KNOWLEDGE PARTNERSHIP

In the summer of 1997, a highly successful conference on using knowledge to fight poverty resulted in a sub-group of the participants setting up a network called the Global Knowledge Partnership (GKP), which has grown and evolved since then to include over 92 member organizations from 40 countries. This community of public, private, and not-for-profit organizations aims to promote broad access to—and effective use of—knowledge and information as tools for sustainable development. A set of partnership principles was agreed, expressed as follows.

Partnership Principles

GKP is committed to an effective partnership as the core of the organization. This requires a clear, mutual understanding of "partnership" which is defined by a simple and easily applicable set of agreed principles.

The effective, genuine partnership contributes to transparent, efficient cooperation and the conscious handling of the relations between institutions.

Core Principles

- *All partners maintain their own identity and autonomy, have equal rights and are enabled to design their own future.*
- *GKP is driven by shared values and mutual respect.*
- *Transparency and trust are essential.*

Working Principles

A central criterion for the partnership and the division of tasks among members is the principle that decisions are taken at the lowest/optimal competent level (see footnote: Subsidiarity).

In managing our partnership, we strike a balance between flexibility at the operational level—which allows the partnership to continuously adapt to a dynamic, rapidly changing context—and continuity at the level of objectives, values and principles, which builds trust and a long term perspective.

We will undertake periodic reviews of partnership values, objectives, principles and benefits.

We live a culture where ...

- *Openness and mutual respect for different opinions are a basis for joint learning processes;*
- *There is readiness to share information and interest to learn from each other;*
- *Benefits of the partnership are accessible to all members on an equal basis;*
- *Clear agreements on values, objectives and principles are established through consultations;*
- *All partner resources are respected equally (i.e., knowledge, experience, human or financial resources).*

Subsidiarity Principle: All responsibilities within an organization are shared equally across the board with the lowest possible level empowered to take action. When functions cannot be implemented more effectively at the lower levels, they will be referred to a higher level.

In addition to its partnership principles, the GKP made it clear what the expectations were of its members, expressed as follows.

Membership Responsibilities

Members are expected to fulfill the roles and responsibilities established by the GKP membership as a whole. The core responsibilities are:
- *Actively initiating and participating in collaborative activities with other partners;*
- *Actively contributing to GKP activities by sharing knowledge and information through the various GKP channels such as: providing links to the GKP Portal; contributing success stories and/or lessons learned to the GKP knowledge base; participating in the virtual marketplace; contributing to "Partners", the monthly GKP Newsletter in the form of links, case study, reports and projects related to the theme; contributing to the GKP ICT for Development Events Calendar;*
- *Regularly attending and contributing to GKP meetings and events;*
- *Participating in and supporting the implementation of the GKP Strategy;*
- *Promoting GKP to facilitate recruitment of new members and outreach efforts.[1]*

Rinalia Abdul Rahim, executive director of GKP and head of the GKP Secretariat, based in Kuala Lumpur, Malaysia, emphasizes the importance of these principles:

> *The responsibilities and principles are particularly important because of the North–South and multi-sectoral nature of the GKP membership. For such a diverse group of organizations to get together, share knowledge, discuss issues, learn from each other and embark on meaningful collaborations towards a shared goal, they need to have shared values, mutual respect, trust and transparency that supports the building of trust. This is critical when organizations bring different types and levels of resources such as knowledge, funds or expertise.*

It can be seen from the example that a charter or statement of principles is completely different from a legal contract. The discussion that produces a collaboration charter is about shared vision, consensus building, commitment, about people holding each other to account—not contractually but morally. Organizations that know how to build collaborative advantage have learnt that trust, moral obligation, goodwill, and enthusiasm for a cause will often produce much greater value for all than the most finely crafted contract pored over by teams of lawyers. Why is this so? For one, it is because human beings give more of their time, energy, and enthusiasm when they feel they have a choice in the matter. Second, a contract can never predict every possible change in the environment that might affect the collaborative effort. One of the major advantages of a group of organizations working together is that collectively they have more antennae picking up changes in the environment than any individual partner would have. One partner, for example, may hear of some proposed legislative changes that could affect the work of a consortium, and bring that to the table for discussion. The consortium may then need to agree some changes in direction, which it can do quickly and without needing to renegotiate any legal terms. Organizations that have gone through the experience of being hamstrung by contracts will know the frustration of needing to renegotiate every step of the way, and the painful delay and cost of armies of lawyers handling these changes. Of course there is still a place for contracts—but that place is largely in the realm of transactional relationships. In the realm of collaboration, goals and principles should be agreed and documented, to help understanding and communication—but beyond this basic foundation the great power of a collaborative effort is its ability to move fast and flexibly as the world around it changes.

Co-location

Just as the importance of the physical environment is often forgotten when meetings are being planned, the opportunity to build a more successful collaboration by locating people at the same site is often missed. There is no question that communication and teamwork are improved if a group of people is based in the same physical location. A large European information technology company once undertook a lessons learnt exercise on the bidding process for a major technology project it had won. The bid team was composed of members from two different organizations who were partnering in order to try and win this particular piece of business. One of the most significant learning points was that the bid team really began to operate as a united team when it was given its own dedicated bid room in one of the partner's office buildings. It was recognized that there had initially been something of a management blind spot on this particular point. The bid team had lobbied for some time before it was allocated the space. The partner organizations had no established process for a collaborative team to request dedicated space (the process only existed for allocating space to employees), they questioned whether the space was really needed, they argued over how the related overhead cost would be paid for, and basically put a significant roadblock in the way of a team that, in theory, was strategically important to the business. This experience emphasizes that in order to establish collaborative advantage, an organization needs both strategic vision and the ability to handle basic, nitty-gritty operational detail in order to help a collaborative group achieve the outcome they want.

Clearly it would not be possible or even appropriate in every case to offer dedicated space to a collaborative venture. However, it is a key question to consider when you are planning collaborative work. It is not just a question of whether co-location would be useful, but what type of physical environment would be most appropriate. It may be important, for example, to site the team somewhere separate to any of the partner organizations' buildings—or even the towns they are located in—in order to help build the collaborative team's sense of identity and to avoid any one organization appearing to have more power than others. The group might need more team meeting space than offices, or perhaps secure storage areas may be required. It might have special IT needs. It might only need the shared space for a limited time. For all these reasons serviced office buildings, with a range of facilities and flexibility on leases, can be a good option to consider.

Ironically, one of the reasons that some organizations resist the idea of co-location is the availability of the information and communication tools that have made collaboration easier in the first place (see Chapter 7 for more on these). Although these tools do make collaboration easier and more cost-effective, they are not a good relationship-building mechanism. They also do not allow those unplanned, serendipitous conversations that take place at lunch in the restaurant or around the coffee machine, or as people pass each other in the corridor. They do not build the sense of team identity that is built when people work together in the same physical space. IT tools have an important role to play, but are not a substitute for face-to-face contact or shared office facilities.

Remember that even if the group is not co-located for the duration of the collaborative effort, the members will need significant face-to-face contact, especially in the early stages, and the choice of environment will be a key consideration. You may wish to consider a compromise option whereby the team members are co-located for a period of weeks or months in the early stages of a collaboration, then return to their home bases once the relationships are well established, at which point other communication methods such as telephone or videoconferencing and email are likely to be more effective.

Ongoing alignment

In this chapter, we have put an emphasis on the early stages of a collaborative relationship, when the initial alignment processes take place. However, the alignment and integration process actually carries on for the duration of the lifecycle of any venture. Previously agreed goals may need to be changed or refined as circumstances change. New members of the team need to be integrated into the group when they join, and their perspectives may modify the agreed goals. We explore more aspects of this ongoing challenge in the next chapter, which examines the process of nurturing a collaborative endeavor over time.

COLLABORATIVE ADVANTAGE CHECKLIST: INTEGRATING THE TEAM AND AGREEING JOINT OUTCOMES

- Have you carefully designed the early meetings so that they help build relationships, develop trust, and clarify joint outcomes?
- Have you ensured all the partners are helping to shape the agenda?
- Have you considered asking an external facilitator to run the meetings so participants can concentrate on content rather than process?
- Have you thought about the physical environment for the meetings, to ensure it adds rather than subtracts from the process?
- Have you built the commitment of the participants to the early meetings to minimize the risks of part-time attendance, delegation, or mismatched expectations?
- Have you discussed with your partners the possibility of creating a collaboration charter to make explicit the rights, responsibilities, and expected behavior of the group members?
- Have you considered the option of co-location, on a temporary or permanent basis?
- Do you have an agreed process for evaluating whether goals need to be refined or changed?

5 Nurturing the Collaborative Process

"Nurturing" is a term not often used in relation to line management, and yet it is an accurate description of one of the major facets of sustaining an effective collaborative process. Of course there are pragmatic steps that one must take in collaborating—to structure the collaboration, allocate resources, project manage key pieces of work. However, the heart of a collaborative effort is a group of human beings, any one of whom can walk away from the process if there is not enough in it for them. Maintaining their enthusiasm and commitment is essential—and enthusiasm and commitment cannot be dictated from above. It can only be nurtured and encouraged, and this needs to happen throughout the lifespan of the collaborative venture.

There are three specific points at which people need particular support and encouragement, which are worthy of special mention:

▶ when they join the collaborative process
▶ when conflicts arise
▶ when the scope of the process needs to be adjusted in light of changed circumstances.

We explore these specific scenarios as well as considering the overall challenges of sustaining the commitment of collaborative partners, including the special challenges of collaborating across cultural as well as organizational boundaries.

Whose job is it?

Before we explore some of the specific issues, it is worth considering whose responsibility it is to nurture the collaborative process. The short answer is that it is the responsibility of everyone involved in the collaboration. Of course some collaborative ventures have an infrastructure of people and processes specifically designed to support them—and in that case those people will take prime responsibility for supporting the participants, ensuring they are in frequent communication with them, and acting on any feedback they may pick up on issues or concerns.

For many collaborative ventures, however, there is no one nominated leader, simply a group of peers working together to achieve something. Picking up the signals that a group member is losing his or her commitment to the process, and then acting quickly to rebuild it is a key skill in a collaborative context. Things to watch out for include:

▶ people being left out or not listened to in team meetings
▶ people contributing a great deal with little thanks or recognition
▶ people no longer attending group meetings as often.

Any member of the collaboration is potentially in a position to help repair the damage. Let us consider a few possible scenarios.

SCENARIOS FOR BUILDING COMMITMENT AND MOTIVATION

If someone's views are not being heard, you could specifically engage them in the conversation:

Robert, I haven't heard your view on this topic, I'd be interested in your perspective.

You may realize that someone has put in a disproportionate amount of effort, and a comment such as this could make all the difference to his or her motivation:

I think it is fantastic that Julie and her team have put in so much time since we last met to pull this information together. Thank you very much for doing that.

You may realize that a member of the partnership has missed the last two meetings. A telephone call to ask why he or she has not been there shows that the person is valued by the group. Even if the absence turns out to be for practical, unavoidable reasons, the telephone call will still be a positive affirmation of the individual's importance to the group. If it turns out that the person is unhappy with how things are developing, the telephone call will get the issue on the table and give the group the opportunity to address the issue.

Because collaborative groups usually do not have traditional line management structures, the chances of achieving success are greatly increased if the group members all consider themselves responsible for the health of the relationships within the group. When you work collaboratively, you need always to be focused on two related dimensions: the task that needs to be achieved, and the relationships with and between the people who need to be engaged and supported in achieving it.

Protecting the core values of the group

After the initial stages of building a collaborative process, the group will have established some ways of working and, either explicitly or implicitly, will have agreed what behavior is either acceptable or not acceptable. These core values are an important touchstone for the group, and need to be communicated and reinforced. These may be clearly articulated within a collaboration charter (described in the previous chapter), but as ever with core values, they are more meaningful when expressed in action rather than words.

One of the greatest enablers of effective collaborative working is this foundation of shared values. Combined with a shared vision of the outcomes you wish to achieve together, you have the basis for success. Many people would argue that shared values cannot be imposed. Therefore the best chance of creating an easy working relationship is to bring people into the process who share the same outlook on life to begin with. Unfortunately, it is not always possible to select the individuals involved in a collaborative process—one simply has to work with the people who have been assigned to it. However, if there is an element of choice, an aspect of nurturing the process is to select individuals who fit in with the shared values of the group.

Jim Collins, co-author of *Built to Last* and *Good to Great*, described the process of bringing new members in to his research team within the research lab that he set up as a joint venture with the University of Colorado.

> *Each person invited to join the team receives a written and verbal orientation on team values, purpose and performance standards and is asked to join only if he or she can commit to those principles. Before joining, each person is told, "If you have any doubt about whether this is the right place for you, then it is in our mutual interest that you decline this opportunity.[1]*

This degree of emphasis on common beliefs at a recruitment stage is relatively unusual in organizational life, although some companies (Hewlett-Packard, for example) are known for the time and attention that they put into the recruitment process. In collaborative working, the recruitment process is key. The importance of selecting the right organizational partners has already been emphasized, and equal importance should be placed on recruiting the right individuals to the process. And although the experience and authority they hold is important, their personal style also matters. Some of the questions that are likely to be relevant in any collaborative situation, when considering potential group members, are as follows:

▶ Do they respect other people's points of view?
▶ Are they able to discuss difficult issues without being defensive or aggressive?
▶ Are they keen to learn from experience?
▶ Do they support and encourage their colleagues?
▶ Do they deliver on their commitments?

These personal qualities will be explored in more detail in Chapter 9. The point to make here is that the collaborative process is likely to be much more difficult to nurture and build if the raw material is a group of people with very different values. If you can influence the choice of individual participants, and if you take the time to induct them effectively into the collaborative environment, you will increase your chances of success significantly.

Consequence management

The process of nurturing the core values of the group has two dimensions: reinforcing them in a positive sense, and ensuring there are consequences if the values are transgressed. For example, a situation could arise where one partner has not respected the confidentiality agreed within the group. An individual might have spoken publicly about an issue that was discussed in confidence within the collaborative setting, for example. What action results? If nothing happens, it is a tacit acceptance of that behavior. If the person is taken to one side and asked to explain his or her actions, the group is reinforcing the value of respecting confidentiality. Better yet, if the situation is discussed publicly at one of the group's meetings, every member of the collaborative venture will become more aware of the importance of respecting that particular value. Common values oil the wheels of collaborative working—without them the process falters and grates. Just as an engineer ensures that a machine has the lubrication it needs to operate smoothly, those responsible for collaborative working need to make sure that common values are understood and respected.

Inducting new joiners

Most organizations recognize that new employees need some form of induction process. These induction processes vary widely in their quality and scope—everything from a standard hour-long briefing from the HR department to a tailored induction program over a number of months, supported by a mentor or coach. An effective induction program, as companies who invest in them know, makes the integration of an employee into the organization's culture and working processes a much more rapid and successful process. The "sink or swim" approach to induction is a much less reliable affair, where new joiners are left to flounder for a time until their knowledge of the organization is sufficient for them to begin to make an effective contribution.

Collaborative ventures, especially those with a limited timescale, cannot afford the "sink or swim" approach when new members join. If induction is not handled effectively, the new participant may subtract from, rather than add value to, the collaborative process. When is induction important? Here are the main scenarios:

▶ When a new partner is invited to join the process.
▶ When one of the existing partners changes its representative or the organizational sponsor.
▶ When one of the current participants delegates his or her participation for a time to a colleague.

An effective induction of a permanent or temporary collaborative partner is not difficult or complicated. The problem is that often it is simply forgotten. As a result people may show up at meetings with no real understanding of what has come before, no relationship with the people who are there, and as a result very little ability to make an effective contribution. This is where a few simple steps can make a big difference.

▶ Identify a "buddy" for the new person who can brief him or her as required, welcome the person to the group, and perform any necessary introductions.
▶ If the person is replacing a previous representative, ensure that the first incumbent does a thorough handover.
▶ Keep a central library of relevant documents, such as the terms of reference of the venture, the collaboration charter, meeting minutes, and contact details of participants, and provide a pack to the new joiner. (There is more on information resources in Chapter 7.)

The Transconstellation Academy, a management development program developed by Solvay Business School in Brussels for a consortium of five specialized financial services firms, occasionally faced difficulties when organizational sponsors from the parent organizations (such as HR directors) changed. Paul Verdin, one of the co-directors of the program, says:

> *This program was the result of two years of discussion between the companies involved. Of course we need to build a relationship with any new person but we decided it would also be helpful to have a written charter that made it clear what had been agreed to date and what the roles and responsibilities were across the consortium. We found this very helpful for any new stakeholders and it avoided them raising lots of questions on aspects of the programme that had already been agreed by their predecessor.*

Treating induction as a core business process for a collaborative venture is simply common sense—but unfortunately not always common practice.

Handling conflict

However well the induction of new members is handled, conflict is bound to develop during any collaborative effort. The steps described above to build a collaborative group with shared values will hopefully minimize the level of conflict, but as with any teambuilding process, the "forming, storming, norming, and performing" sequence[2] is likely to apply—and the "storming" phase, like it or not, is an inevitable one.

Conflicts can arise for a number of reasons. Among the most common are:

▶ personality conflicts
▶ differences of views on goals or strategies
▶ tensions over allocation of costs and benefits
▶ lack of clarity on roles and responsibilities.

One of the greatest threats to a collaborative process is a conflict left unresolved. One simple method that can defuse tension is to ensure that at every meeting of the group, a standard topic on the agenda is the working process of the group. This gives all of the group members permission to raise difficulties or tensions before they become insurmountable.

Some interpersonal conflict is best handled one-to-one rather than publicly within the group. However, it should be possible for any member of the group to suggest that the two (or more) parties involved hold a frank conversation. Again, the principle here is shared ownership of the success of the collaborative process.

When serious conflict arises, this is another time at which it can be useful to consider bringing in an external facilitator. Depending on the reasons for the conflict, it can be very helpful to have someone from outside the process, with no vested interest other than helping the group to move forward, brought in to ensure that the difficult issues are put on the table and resolved. An example follows in the box.

THE STORY OF PSL

In 1990 the UK government's Department for Trade and Industry and the business network CBI (Confederation of British Industry) established a not-for-profit organization called Partnership Sourcing Ltd or PSL, whose aim was to promote the concept and practice of partnering in business. Although PSL has a strong focus on collaborative forms of customer–supplier relationships in particular, its work is relevant to the building of many forms of business relationship. Much of their effort is centered on helping different organizations build the capability to partner more effectively with others.

In one case PSL was called in when two partner organizations were close to taking each other to court. One was a major national service provider and the other a supplier to it of some important technology for an automated distribution centre. Although their relationship was described as a partnership, the relationship between the two firms had in fact broken down. PSL was brought in as an objective external advisor to assess the situation and help the partners find a way forward.

At the heart of the issue, PSL identified a traditional, confrontational attitude to customer–supplier relationships, a tendency towards a blame culture when things went wrong, and several interpersonal clashes. PSL asked the members of the partnership team from both organizations to provide input on their views of the state of the relationship. The consolidated set of results was shared at the start of a joint workshop to address the issues. By demonstrating the value of open communication and getting the major issues out on the table, this enabled some of the emotion to be taken out of the situation, and the group started on a more constructive path. After a detailed action plan had been agreed, the partnership was back on solid ground, and as a significant indicator of progress, the next major milestone in the project implementation plan was met successfully.

Setting an expectation that conflict will arise—and agreeing that the aim is to handle it more effectively each time it arises—is a good challenge for a collaborative group. Just as customer-focused businesses try to view every customer complaint as an opportunity to build an even stronger customer relationship, every conflict in a collaborative setting is an opportunity to make the partnership even stronger and more effective.

Reviewing and adjusting the scope

Another of the common conflict points is the process of agreeing specific goals for the collaborative process. With participants bringing different organizational and personal wins to the table, it is inevitable that differences of opinion will arise. The process of building consensus was covered in Chapter 4. However it is important to bear in mind that a collaboration is a process from which new ideas and directions emerge as the group develops. The need to review the scope and goals of the group is an ongoing process that should be considered a natural part of collaborative working, rather than a sign of failure or weakness.

Herein lies one of the differences between a transactional relationship and a collaborative one. In a transactional relationship, the goal is usually fixed—for example, to deliver a particular service to a certain set of standards and at a particular cost. In collaborative working, the process generally starts off with a stated desire to find outcomes of mutual benefit, and the specific goals emerge as the process unfolds. Some individuals will be uncomfortable with this dynamic of evolving aims. What are the measurable outcomes, they may ask, when you seek their commitment to joining a collaborative process. The reality is that at the start there may only be some very broad objectives—and the ones that are initially agreed will inevitably change.

The principle of equity for all of the partners is one that can influence the scope of the venture. For example, shifting to a new aim might benefit several of the partners and penalize another one. To avoid this becoming a conflict, the skill is to ensure that the losers are either compensated in some way for the negative impact, or convinced that it is worth it for a longer-term gain. Collaboration inevitably involves give and take.

Many unexpected events in the wider world may affect the scope of the venture. New legislation, new competitors, new technologies, political decisions: one of the advantages of collaborative working is having more antennae to sense changes in the environment and respond quickly and appropriately. As long as the venture is not trapped within a contractual framework that prevents flexibility, the ability to shift focus quickly can be one of the greatest benefit of working with others. Setting expectations with group members that the scope will change over time—and handling those changes in scope equitably for all participants—is one of the key processes within a collaborative venture.

In Chapter 4 it was recommended that the initial goals of the collaborative effort be documented. That discipline should be maintained as the scope shifts over time. Collaborative ventures may not need complicated legal frameworks, but this does not mean that agreed goals should not be documented. To avoid misunderstanding and to support any induction processes for new members, the scope of the venture needs to be tracked— in writing—as it evolves.

Recognizing individual contributions

As part of the structuring process covered in Chapter 3, costs and benefits need to be allocated fairly between the partners. This is the tangible aspect of reward. However, the nurturing process includes the need to recognize the contributions of individual participants in the collaborative process— a form of intangible reward. The success of a collaborative venture often requires investment in time and energy by individual members which, at a particular point in time, do not necessarily lead to a tangible reward. Perhaps someone works over a weekend to help the venture to meet a key deadline. Someone makes his or her team's meeting room available for a key event. Or perhaps one of the partners brings in a whole team of people to complete a piece of work that requires their skills. Any one of these contributions deserves recognition, whether or not they directly relate to a tangible reward. Knowing when and how to say "thank you" is a vital part of the nurturing process.

Ending a collaboration

If you have prepared a collaboration carefully, you will have agreed an exit strategy up front, covering the main things that will happen if and when the collaboration comes to an end. Sometimes things will go entirely according to plan, with the partners reaching the natural end of the collaboration, and the exit strategy implemented as agreed. More often than not however, unexpected events lead to a premature end to the collaborative venture. Whatever the circumstances, the aim of all partners should be to exit the collaboration with goodwill and trust still intact. For one thing, one never knows when a partnership might be re-established. Second, it will be difficult to establish new partnerships if previous partners are negative about the experience of working with you.

One important step is to bring positive closure to the venture, perhaps through a form of celebration. Whether this is a social event or a formal ceremony of some kind, it should be designed as a way of thanking the contributors, celebrating the success achieved, learning lessons from the difficulties, and moving forward with a positive outlook.

Working across cultures

It is worth noting that there are special challenges involved in nurturing a collaborative process that involves people from different cultures. In one sense everything we have considered so far is an example of cross-cultural working, in that organizations have different cultures. However there is clearly another layer of complexity when the individuals concerned have a different cultural background as well, which is most commonly found in collaborations that span national boundaries.

In addition to the skills involved in nurturing the relationships between a set of human beings from one national culture, there is significant skill involved in creating easy working relationships between people from entirely different cultures. It can be beneficial to build some cross-cultural education into the induction process, if cross-cultural working is a strong feature of the collaborative venture. Culture clashes and misunderstandings can occur across a broad spectrum of issues, such as:

▶ language
▶ time management
▶ meeting styles
▶ knowing when a commitment is a commitment
▶ who decides what
▶ speed and form of decision-making
▶ status.

If the people involved in a venture have a great deal of international experience, they are likely to be sensitive to these issues, and culture clashes will therefore be reduced. If they are new to international working, or to working with a particular culture, investment in some cross-cultural education may be worthwhile. There are a number of training providers across the world that offer briefings on working with other cultures, and a number of books on cross-cultural working which are also useful preparation.[3]

Valuing scarce skills

Maintaining a positive, high-performing collaboration is a significant achievement. As will be clear by now, there are many obstacles and difficulties that can get in the way. Any process that is centered on a group of human beings will be unpredictable, with unintended or unexpected consequences for every action that is taken. It is essential to have people within the group (and at times external help) who understand group dynamics and know how to handle the difficulties and breakdowns that inevitably occur. Successfully guiding a collaborative venture through the minefield of interpersonal conflict, political whims, potential culture clashes, and a range of other unexpected obstacles takes skill, courage, and determination. People with a track record of successfully steering a group through the minefield have a capability that should be greatly valued.

COLLABORATIVE ADVANTAGE CHECKLIST: NURTURING THE COLLABORATIVE PROCESS

■ Do all those involved in the collaborative effort consider themselves responsible for effective working relationships within the group?
■ Have the core values of the group been agreed and articulated?
■ Are clear actions taken to reinforce common values, including clear consequences when they are transgressed?
■ Is care taken, where possible, to select individual members who are naturally collaborative in their approach?
■ Are there established induction processes for new joiners or temporary joiners?
■ Are there established conflict prevention processes, such as reviewing the working relationships at every meeting?
■ Are there agreed means of handling conflicts that arise, such as bringing in an external facilitator?
■ Is there training available on cross-cultural working, if needed?
■ Does the group have a conscious aim to continually improve the way it deals with conflict?
■ Is the scope of the collaborative effort kept under regular review and modified as required?
■ Are any changes to the scope and aims of the venture documented and shared with relevant stakeholders, including all members of the group?
■ Are contributions to the collaborative venture recognized informally at a personal level as well as formally rewarded at an organizational level?

6 Resourcing the Collaborative Effort

For want of a nail, the shoe was lost.
For want of a shoe, the horse was lost.
For want of a horse, the rider was lost.
For want of a rider, the battle was lost.
For want of a battle, the kingdom was lost.
And all for the want of a horseshoe nail.

This children's nursery rhyme is one way of summarizing a common pitfall in relation to collaborative working. Sometimes the lack of one or two very simple things can scupper the whole venture. It is perhaps stating the obvious, but collaborative working requires resources. Because of the coordination required, it often takes greater resources than an initiative run by one organization. Strangely, there appears to be something of a management blind spot when it comes to ensuring that collaborative efforts have the staffing and money they require. The same people who ensure that their organization's own projects have the necessary allocation of budget and people are often guilty of expecting their representatives on a collaborative effort to make it work with no dedicated budget and no additional resources. Collaborative working is often implicitly positioned as an optional extra, something you do on top of the "day job." Only now are organizations beginning to realize that collaborative efforts often are the day job for their representatives—or if they are not, they should be.

Cross-organizational resourcing

Successfully resourcing a collaborative effort is not a straightforward process. Most resource allocation processes are designed to fit within the boundaries of one organization—in fact, they are generally designed to support one department or function within one organization, with budget cost centres allocated to particular managers. When a number of organizations come together to achieve something jointly, their resource allocation processes often sit uncomfortably alongside the resource needs of the collaborative venture.

There are two major aspects to resourcing a collaborative effort that need consideration. These are resourcing the collaborative process itself, and resourcing joint initiatives. Let us consider each of these in turn.

Resourcing the collaborative process

Just as any project needs a project management infrastructure, a collaborative venture needs a collaboration infrastructure. The form this infrastructure takes will depend on the scope and structure of the venture. In cases where a collaboration is set up as a separate legal entity, the resourcing requirement may be significant, as it is in effect the start-up of a new company. In situations where the collaboration is not set up as a separate legal entity, there are still a number of aspects to the collaborative process that will need resourcing if the venture is to be successful.

In essence, there are three major forms of coordination for a collaborative process:

FACILITATED COLLABORATION

This applies to collaborative ventures where there is an infrastructure specifically allocated to coordinating the collaboration. In facilitated collaboration, the dedicated coordination resource is a support function, providing coordination and facilitation to enable a group of partners to achieve specific aims. The main distinction from the next category, structural coordination, is that the support function is not held accountable for the end result.

For example, a management development consultancy might facilitate a management development program for a consortium of companies. This is an example of companies collaborating for the purpose of learning. However the responsibility for putting that learning to good use rests with the companies involved. The management development consultancy cannot be accountable for the ultimate outcome, although it is of course accountable for providing an effective service that meets the requirements of the stakeholder companies.

STRUCTURAL COLLABORATION

In this model, an infrastructure (often a legal entity) is set up to be responsible for the venture, with specific individuals—such as a board, chief executive and staff of a specially designed legal entity—held accountable for the agreed outcomes.

For example, a joint venture company with a board of directors and an executive management team is a form of structural collaboration, with the accountability for achieving results lying firmly within the governance structure that has been established. It is important that the resourcing process takes into account the additional coordination required for a process that brings together a number of organizations.

SELF-MANAGED COLLABORATION

Here the coordination of the collaborative effort is managed by the partners involved, with no separate entity established. There are many different ways in which this can be achieved, with different partners contributing different skills and resources and the costs being distributed as appropriate.

For example, a network of community organizations might work together to deliver a better overall service to their community. Due to limited resources, they might share the tasks of organizing, chairing, and hosting meetings and distribute agreed actions as they arise to the most suitable person within a partner organization.

All three forms have advantages and disadvantages, and the choice will depend on the aims and scope of the particular venture. However, all three models encompass a similar range of core resource requirements to support the collaboration process itself, and these are outlined in the box.

CORE COLLABORATION RESOURCES

Managerial resource to oversee the venture. This may be one person or several acting as a board or steering group. Depending on the scope of the venture, the managerial infrastructure may also include a number of gatekeeper roles to manage relationships with different stakeholders.

Coordination resource to manage the day-to-day operations of the collaborative venture. This is typically a more hands-on role, which supports the leadership role(s) and usually directs the work of the administrative support function. In smaller collaborative ventures the same person or people may take on the leadership and coordination roles.

Administrative resource to support the organization of the collaboration—

organizing meetings, supporting the information technology requirements of the group, facilitating communication flows, maintaining information resources such as websites and libraries, and overseeing accounting processes. This crucial role (or roles) is a great enabler to effective collaborative working, and is often forgotten or undervalued when new ventures are being planned.

Facilitator(s) to design and run meetings, workshops, and conferences. In some collaborative ventures, the coordinator and facilitator roles are one and the same. In self-managed collaboration, the facilitation role may be shared amongst the partners. Facilitation can be something called upon for specific reasons at particular times in the venture's development, or alternatively it may be a permanent support function.

In terms of actually filling these roles, a number of models can be considered:

▶ People are hired into these coordination roles within some form of legal entity, and the costs are shared between the partners according to a model seen as equitable by them.
▶ Several partners nominate people to fulfill these different roles. They remain employed by their original organization, and form a virtual team. These assignments are factored into the balance of costs and benefits.
▶ One of the partners offers to undertake the main coordination roles, and that service is factored into the cost–benefit model for the venture. This model runs the risk of one partner being seen as having more power than others.
▶ An external organization is contracted to provide one or more of the coordination roles, and the costs of this service are shared between the collaborating organizations. This organization may be providing similar services to other collaborative efforts.
▶ In self-managed collaboration, the coordination roles are allocated on an *ad hoc* basis to different people, as the need arises.

The important lesson is that collaboration needs coordination. To achieve collaborative advantage, people with the relevant skills and the requisite time available need to be in place to fulfill these coordination roles. Without them, the venture has a much lower probability of success.

Resourcing the initiatives of the collaborative venture

So far we have focused on resourcing the collaborative process itself. There is also clearly a need to resource the projects and activities that the collaborative group decides to undertake. Depending on the activities chosen, a wide variety of skills may be required. The challenge that arises in a collaborative setting is the pragmatic question of how to resource these joint activities. The choices are similar to the ones noted above in relation to the coordination responsibilities, namely:

▶ *Recruitment model:* hire someone to take on the role, sharing costs between the partners.
▶ *Lead partner model:* one partner takes a lead role for a particular piece of work, and resources that project.
▶ *Secondment model:* activities are resourced using appropriate people, full or part-time, from the partner organizations.
▶ *Contractor model:* external resources are contracted to provide the services to the collaborative venture.
▶ *Ad hoc model:* as specific needs arise, different partners identify people in their organizations who can do a particular piece of work.

Whichever resourcing model is used, a funding method needs to be agreed. This will depend on the accounting model set up for the venture, but one way or another, these resources need to be paid for. In some cases a central pot may be established to fund joint working, and partner organizations that second people to the venture will charge their people's time to that budget; while in other cases, the partners may agree that contributions from their staff are counted as part of their contribution to the venture without actual money changing hands. Either way, the delicate balance of costs and benefits will be affected by these resourcing decisions.

Organizations new to collaborative working often expect the organizational participants to fulfill all of these roles as part-time responsibilities. This may be possible for small-scale collaborative efforts, but generally this is setting the process up to fail. If the strategic analysis has been done and the value of the collaborative effort has been clearly established, it is important to ensure that the process is appropriately resourced. If it is not possible to find the required resources to ensure that the collaborative process works smoothly, it is preferable not to embark on the process in the first place. The goodwill that may initially carry an under-resourced venture will eventually wear thin, and the end result will be frustration and disappointment, as a collaboration with good potential grinds to a halt, simply because the participants do not have enough time to maintain the health of the collaboration and fulfill their commitments to it.

The choice of how much resource to apply to the collaborative effort is again context-specific. The pros and cons of the various approaches are summarized in Table 6.1.

Table 6.1 **Resourcing strategies**

Resourcing strategy	Applicability	Benefits	Disadvantages
Recruitment model	Useful for collaborative efforts with significant coordination requirements. Resources typically include managerial, administrative, facilitation and/or project management resources. Dedicated office space may also be required.	Reduces investment of time and effort needed from individual partners.Improves communication flows. Dedicated to monitoring and supporting the success of the collaborative effort with no conflicting priorities.	More costly and time-consuming than other approaches. Funding mechanism needs to be determined. Question of who employs the dedicated resources if collaboration is not set up as a separate legal entity. Need to determine what happens to the people if/when venture is wound up.
Lead partner model	Same as for recruitment model.	Simpler than seconding people from different organizations.Team works within one organizational structure with common processes. No need to recruit new people.	Can have conflicts of priorities if lead partner does not dedicate resources to the collaborative venture. Financial and charging model needed in relation to the cost involved. Lead partner can be perceived as more powerful than others within the collaborative group.
Secondment model (full-time or part-time)	Same as for recruitment model.	No need to recruit new people. Secondees have known capabilities. Helps build shared sense of ownership and involvement of partner organizations. Secondees have a home organization to return to when venture finishes.	Additional burden of filling secondees' roles while they are on secondment. Question of which partners provide secondees. Financial model needed to ensure seconding organizations are recognized as having made this contribution, with an appropriate charging model as required. Part-time secondees may have conflicting priorities.

Table 6.1 **continued**

Resourcing strategy	Applicability	Benefits	Disadvantages
Contractor model	Same as for recruitment and secondment models.	Rapid implementation as team, process and infrastructure are already in place, ready to support the venture. Simple to stop when the venture finishes. Depending on organization chosen, it may have significant experience of facilitating collaborative work.	Contractor may support other partnerships at the same time so conflicts of priorities sometimes arise. Contractor is accountable for supporting the venture well but cannot be held accountable for actual outcomes.
Ad hoc model	Suitable for small scale collaborative efforts, preferably with established relationships.	No additional cost. May help to encourage a sense of shared ownership of the collaborative process.	Collaborative effort often not viewed as part of the "day job" and may not get necessary priority or the right skills applied. People may not be recognized by their home organization for the contribution they make.

Project management

One of the most common roles required to support collaborative initiatives is that of a project manager. As specific actions or programs of work are agreed, it is almost always essential to have a nominated individual responsible for driving those actions through. Again, this is often overlooked. As an illustration of the value that a project manager can bring, the box has a story of a community initiative that highlights the role of a project manager as a critical success factor.

THE STORY OF THE DAVENTRY PARTNERSHIP

Across the United Kingdom, local government authorities were initially encouraged and then required by central government to establish local strategic partnerships (or LSPs). An LSP is designed to bring together the main organizational players that serve a particular town or district, in order to develop an effective and well-coordinated community strategy. Typically the members of an LSP include the local authority, the emergency services, the health service, voluntary organizations, and representatives of the business community.

Many early attempts at LSPs were found to be ineffective, as they rarely invested in the relationship building and alignment processes that we now know to be crucial to collaborative working. LSP members often sent different representatives to the infrequent meetings of the LSP, and the agenda was largely driven by the local authority, which had a vested interest in being seen to make the LSP happen. Not surprisingly, very little of significance emerged from this style of working.

A small district in central England decided it would try a different approach. The elected leader of the council and the chief executive of Daventry District Council commissioned some external help with designing and facilitating a process of gaining alignment between interested LSP members for some early collaborative wins. They committed themselves to five two-day workshops over a six-month period to determine which joint actions to take, and to develop the relevant action plans. Although ten days may not sound like much, this required enormous commitment from a group of busy people. Ten members of the LSP, which had approximately 30 organizations as members in total, came together to experiment with this new approach. They chose two pilot projects to test their collaborative process. One was an information service to the local citizens, and the second was a crime reduction initiative targeting young people in the area. Both projects required significant coordination between different community organizations.

Initially the LSP members relied on each other to take necessary actions between meetings. However it soon became clear that this would not be enough to enable them to deliver results. After the first two workshops they appointed a dedicated project manager (seconded from the local authority) to oversee the two pilot projects. All participants agreed that without this step they would have been unable to make much further progress.

Project managers who are engaged to support a collaborative venture need to be very effective at stakeholder management. They will need to deliver on agreed outcomes while balancing sometimes conflicting requirements from different partner organizations.

Operating expenses

So far the principal focus of this chapter has been on the allocation of people to collaborative tasks. Clearly it is not just people's time that needs funding in a collaborative setting. Depending on the scope of the venture, a wide range of other activities may need to have budget allocated to them. Although it would be impossible to list every conceivable resource needed for a collaborative process, it may be useful to share some of the main costs that are likely to affect most collaborative ventures in some shape or form, in addition to people costs. These are as follows.

COMMON OPERATING EXPENSES

▶ **Travel expenses—transport, hotels.**
▶ **Meeting facilities—rooms, meals.**
▶ **Office space.**
▶ **Office supplies.**
▶ **Office services such as word processing, photocopying, message taking.**
▶ **Web site design and maintenance and other IT-related costs.**
▶ **Marketing costs, for example logo design, stationery, business cards.**
▶ **Telephone and/or video-conferencing.**

The first two items, travel expenses and meeting facility costs, are essential to factor into the collaborative venture's budget. Meeting face-to-face will always be an important aspect of collaborative work, and it is surprising how often a collaborative venture can run into difficulty because no one is expecting or prepared to pay for the cost of getting people into the same room. These costs can of course be covered in several ways—for example, paid for by the partners actually traveling to meetings, or paid for out of a central budget. Either way, the cost of meeting needs to be factored in to the resourcing process. The wider the geographical scope of the venture, the higher this cost will be—but it is a fundamental aspect of collaborative working, and should be viewed as an investment in the success of the venture rather than an avoidable cost. The view that electronic or telephone communication can substitute for face-to-face meetings is misguided. Of course a range of communication methods can be used at different points but face-to-face time is essential, especially in the early relationship-building phase of a collaborative effort.

In some collaborative ventures, the people participating in the process have roles that need to be covered while they are contributing to the collaborative work. For example, UK-based charity Macmillan Cancer Relief works with a range of family doctors or general practitioners (GPs) in order to further the doctors' knowledge of managing care and providing services for people affected by cancer. Macmillan funds the time of these GPs through what is known as "backfill," namely the cost of providing a locum doctor to cover for the GP while he or she is working with Macmillan. When these GPs attend Macmillan meetings, workshops, or conferences, Macmillan also pays for their travel expenses. Without Macmillan's financial contribution in these areas, it would simply not be possible for these busy doctors to devote their time to working with Macmillan, and other GPs to improve the services provided to people affected by cancer. Despite being committed to the same outcomes, namely effective patient care, the people involved in this particular collaborative effort need the financial support of a sponsoring organization to be able to contribute.

Goodwill and commitment to shared aims are necessary but not sufficient. Building collaborative advantage requires investment.

Venture capital

Some collaborative ventures build in the ability to fund specific projects by allocating a sum of money as a kind of venture capital fund. Partners in the collaborative venture put proposals forward, and if they fulfill the appropriate criteria, they are allocated some funds from the budget set aside for that purpose. The box gives one example from the field of higher education.

A STORY FROM FIVE COLLEGES INC.

In Chapter 3, we shared the story of Five Colleges Inc., a consortium of five higher education institutions (four liberal arts colleges and a state university) in western Massachusetts which have collaborated for close to 50 years. Five Colleges Inc., which coordinates the consortium, is set up as a non-profit institution, with a staff of 16 headed by executive director Lorna Peterson.

Five Colleges Inc. has three principal funds from which faculty members can bid for project money. These are:

▶ The Seminar Fund: enables faculty groups to host seminars of specialized topics of interest in their field. Typically funds 25–30 faculty seminars a year.
▶ The Lecture Fund: funds symposia and conferences, which must be supported by at least three of the five member institutions. Based on a matched funding principle in relation to contributions from the member institutions.
▶ The Humanities Fund and the Neill Fund: two endowment funds used for joint faculty development and appointments.

In addition to bidding for funds from these existing resources, faculty groups can propose joint projects to the Deans Council and, ultimately, the Board of Directors. For example, the African Studies faculty committee wanted to invite scholars from Africa to visit the five colleges, both to further their careers and to give Five College students the opportunity to learn from them. They put this proposal to the Deans Council and the Board of Directors, and were given the

---

go-ahead to develop the project, with the caveat that the faculty committee would need to find the necessary funding. With the help of one of the college presidents and the Five Colleges Inc. staff, the funding was found and the project went ahead.

The Five Colleges Inc. staff also plays a key role in bidding for grants from public and private sources. These grants now account for approximately 35–40 percent of the operating budget. Grant money is often used for joint faculty appointments or curriculum development. When the grants run out, typically after one to three years, Five Colleges Inc. faces the challenge of gaining commitment to longer-term institutional funding for the initiatives that have longer-term value. For example, a shared foreign language resource centre was initially established with a grant, and continues to be funded through the member institutions. Joint faculty, whose first years might be funded through a grant, have a home institution that employs them and typically funds half of their salary. The faculty member will teach for roughly half their time at the home institution and share the rest of his or her time between the other four institutions.

Executive director Lorna Peterson says:

There are inevitably tensions over money, such as when budget cuts are being required at member institutions. They then expect to see cuts in our budget too. But the Seminar Fund, for example, has been one of the most valued processes that we have put in place. The opportunity to share ideas and experience with a wider group of faculty members from a specialist area is a major attraction of joining a Five Colleges member institution.

Intangible contributions

The resources we have covered so far are tangible—mainly people and money. However it is important to recognize that a partner organization can bring intangible resources to a collaborative effort. For example, a powerful organization with high credibility in its sector can bring the power and influence of its brand to a collaborative effort, which may be worthwhile even if it puts less money or fewer people into the venture than other partners do. Another organization may have some key political relationships, which could open doors that would not otherwise be open. These intangible contributions are important to take into account, as they may bring as much benefit as the more tangible ones.

The role of the public sector

Governments can play an important role in providing funds to enable collaboration to take place. Many public-sector bodies fund collaborative research, for example. Unfortunately some of these publicly funded initiatives get bogged down in bureaucracy, and deliver less value than expected. Some inspiration can be taken from the example of the Australian government, which has funded a Cooperative Research Centres Programme that has operated since 1990. After a number of formal evaluations, the CRC Programme is still going strong, having delivered real value across a wide range of sectors. The CRC story is told in the box.

THE STORY OF THE AUSTRALIAN COOPERATIVE RESEARCH CENTRES

The Cooperative Research Centres Programme is administered by the Department of Education, Science and Training of the Australian government, with a clear aim to improve the commercialization and utilization of research and development.[1] Partnerships between researchers and industry are given the possibility of applying for funding from the Australian government to support collaborative efforts that focus on both research and adoption of that research. The breadth of topics covered in the 158 CRCs selected over nine selection rounds is demonstrated by this brief selection of examples:

▶ CRC for Aboriginal and Tropical Health.
▶ CRC for Molecular Plant Breeding.
▶ CRC for Water Quality and Treatment.
▶ CRC for Cochlear Implant and Hearing Aid Innovation.
▶ CRC for Clean Power from Lignite.
▶ CRC for Technology Enabled Capital Markets.
▶ CRC for Construction Innovation.

The main sectors covered by the CRCs are agriculture, information and communication technology, mining and energy, medical science, environment, and manufacturing technology. An assessment panel judges the applications put forward, and awards funding for up to seven years, on the basis that each CRC will match or exceed the government's funding with cash or in-kind contributions. By the end of 2004 more than A$9.6 billion had been committed to CRCs in both cash and in-kind resources, showing the magnitude of the commitment from a wide range of stakeholders.

The length of funding (up to seven years, and with the possibility of applying for further funding for collaborative projects that emerge from existing CRCs) and the direct involvement of research users in the research have been important success factors. A CRC collaboration must include at least one Australian higher education institution and at least one private sector participant, but these are the only criteria imposed on CRC membership constitution. Also, CRCs are permitted to add or substitute participants over the lifetime of the CRC, building in a flexibility that other more bureaucratic approaches might not tolerate. There is no upper or lower limit to funding levels, each proposal being assessed on its own merits.

Each CRC puts its own governance structure in place, although CRCs are now being asked to set up as incorporated entities unless otherwise agreed.

The Cooperative Research Centres Association (CRCA)[2] was established in 1994 to give a national voice to the many CRCs, and to act as a forum for sharing ideas and experience for what is now a significant community of people and organizations.

Depending on the focus of a particular collaboration, there may be a range of possible sources of funding which can at least pump-prime the activity. The public sector is an obvious possible source of funds, as are charitable foundations or corporate sponsors. It is worth investigating such options at the preparation phase, as these sources of funding may make the difference between being able to achieve a successful outcome and not even getting off the starting block.

The value of pragmatism

One of the qualities of people who lead collaborative efforts successfully is the ability to balance strategic vision with pragmatism. Having a well-crafted vision and a group of committed partners is necessary but not sufficient to achieve desired outcomes. All of the standard managerial challenges of implementation also apply. Knowing what resources it will take to make something happen is an essential component of a collaborative effort. Finding and funding resources is a complex process in a collaborative setting, in view of the range of possible resourcing models and the challenge of fitting the chosen model with the resourcing processes of partner organizations. This is an aspect of collaborative working that should not be underestimated.

COLLABORATIVE ADVANTAGE CHECKLIST: RESOURCING THE COLLABORATIVE EFFORT

- Do the partners have a shared understanding of the different resourcing models, and have they discussed which one (or ones) is most appropriate for this venture?
- Has the collaboration process itself been allocated the appropriate coordination resources?
- Have the different work packages agreed by the collaborative venture been resourced appropriately?
- Have the resource contributions (both tangible and intangible) of different partners been recognized in the allocation of costs and benefits?
- Is there a financial accounting model that enables costs to be allocated as required?
- Have all of the costs of the venture been identified and the appropriate funding mechanisms agreed between the partners?
- Would it be beneficial to put in place one or more central funds to enable member organizations to fund specific initiatives? If so, which criteria should be applied to any bids?
- Are there any funding sources that could be approached to help support the initiative, for example public sector organizations, charitable foundations, or corporate sponsors?

7 Communicating and Sharing Information

The importance of face-to-face meetings in collaborative work has already been emphasized. However, there will inevitably be significant time between physical meetings, when it is important to keep the communication channels open between the partners in a collaborative venture. Also, the venture will, over time, build up an information base that will be useful to all partners as the work progresses. Communication and information sharing are vital processes in collaborative work, for the following reasons:

▶ the need to communicate with a wide range of stakeholders, both those directly involved in the collaboration and others such as the organizational sponsors
▶ the need for working groups to communicate with each other on specific projects or initiatives
▶ the need to have a shared information repository for general use, to avoid duplication of effort or wasted time looking for information.

In order to develop effective communication processes, it is important to pay attention to both what needs to be communicated and how it can best be communicated, which brings us on to the role of information and communication technology.

The role of information and communication technology

A range of information and communication technology applications are useful to support collaboration. The most commonly used tools are highlighted in the box overleaf.

INFORMATION AND COMMUNICATION TECHNOLOGY TOOLS TO SUPPORT COLLABORATION

There are two main types of technology tools to support collaboration, asynchronous and synchronous. Asynchronous technologies enable partners to collaborate by communicating at different times, which can be especially useful if they are collaborating across time zones or have schedules that are difficult to coordinate. Synchronous technologies enable partners to collaborate by communicating in real time, but without having to be physically located in the same place.

Asynchronous technologies

▶ Email: one-to-one or one-to-many communication.
▶ Email distribution lists/listserv: an alternative to a discussion forum (see below) using email technology.
▶ Document management systems: track document versions securely.
▶ Project management tools: ensure all members of the project team have up-to-date information.
▶ Discussion groups, newsgroups, message boards, forums: these give the ability to post questions and responses, and everyone can see both the questions and replies (unlike standard email). These are sometimes moderated.
▶ Shared calendars: make it easier to arrange meetings.
▶ Information repositories: somewhere (often a website) where documents can be held for general use (but without the security and version control capabilities of document management systems).
▶ Workflow applications: software that tracks a document through a particular business or consultation process.

Synchronous technologies

▶ Telephone conferencing: an effective way of connecting people in different places.
▶ Videoconferencing: adds a visual element but generally less effective (and more expensive) than telephone conferencing.
▶ Web or data conferencing: enables people to view shared information on their computer screen while also being able to speak to each other (either by phone or Internet).
▶ Instant messaging and chat rooms: a facility for communicating electronically to other people who are online at the same time.

In addition there are other more specialized applications, such as collaborative computer-aided design (CAD) systems.

An extensive number of products are now being badged as "collaborative software," so professional help and advice on selecting the right product(s) may be useful. Bear in mind that a great deal can be achieved with telephone conferencing, email, and somewhere to store and access shared information, all of which should be possible without any significant investment in technology.

Dispelling the myths

There are many misconceptions about the role of technology in supporting collaboration, and before looking at the positive applications of technology, it is worth dispelling some of the myths.

MYTH NUMBER ONE: IF YOU ARE ABLE TO COMMUNICATE ELECTRONICALLY, YOU WILL NOT NEED TO MEET FACE-TO-FACE

This is one of the most common and most damaging myths of all. As has been stressed, the foundation of effective collaborative working is trust and good working relationships. These cannot be established remotely. As the managing director of a large business network stated, "Trust gets built in the wine and cheese space."[1] Once good working relationships are established, technology tools can certainly be put to good use to facilitate communication. Until that foundation is there, however, there can be no substitute for face-to-face meetings. And because of the importance of nurturing those relationships on an ongoing basis, one or two early meetings will not be enough to do the trust-building job. Effective collaboration involves a mixture of face-to-face and virtual communication, and knowing which approach to take at a particular point in time.

Some people assert that it is much more cost-effective to use virtual communication rather than face-to-face meetings. The response to that stance is simple: something inexpensive that does not get the desired result is not more cost-effective. It is simply a waste of time and money.

MYTH NUMBER TWO: IF YOU PROVIDE TECHNOLOGY TOOLS, PEOPLE WILL USE THEM

You may remember a 1989 film entitled *Field of Dreams*, which starred Kevin Costner and included the memorable line "If you build it, they will come." Unfortunately, with regard to a wide range of collaborative technology tools, the opposite is true. You may well provide a website, a discussion forum, a chat facility, or a document management system to the partners in a collaborative venture—and indeed all of these technologies can play a role in facilitating collaborative work. However, there is a consistent tendency to underestimate the time and effort required to get people to use a technology tool with which they are not familiar. Even if they are computer literate, the adoption of any new tool is a change to their working practices, and requires coaching and encouragement. There has to be a clear benefit to the individual to shift to the new way of working—and doing it "for the greater good" is simply not enough of a motivation. Just making a tool available does not guarantee usage. If it saves people time or makes their job easier, however, it has a good chance of success.

Some years ago oil company BP introduced desktop videoconferencing as a way of ensuring it had global access to scarce technical skills, which might be located on an oil rig in the North Sea at a time when they were needed elsewhere in the company. "Globally available local experts" was the tag line used, within a project known as the Virtual Teamwork project. The technology enabled someone in one country to communicate with a technical expert many miles away, with voice and image appearing on the desktop computer. The project team that deployed this particular technology were quite clear on how to allocate the project budget, namely with more money allocated to an awareness campaign and one-to-one coaching program than to the acquisition of the technology itself. The success of the project was attributed to this unusual split of resources. The same sort of philosophy should be applied when a collaborative venture decides to deploy a new technology tool across the group of partner organizations. The main question should not be, "What tool shall we use?" but rather "How will we get this tool into active use?"

MYTH NUMBER THREE: IT IS USEFUL TO CAPTURE EVERYTHING IN IT SYSTEMS

Because there is now such limitless capacity to store information, there can be a tendency to suggest that every single document related to a collaborative venture needs to be stored in a database. Bear in mind that most people are struggling with information overload rather than a lack of information. A collaborative venture should make some strategic decisions about which information to generate, keep, and share, and ensure that its information architecture meets the needs of the group. (See below for guidance on how to establish an effective information architecture.) If too much information is collected, people begin to find it difficult to find what they want. The natural tendency then is to give up on the databases and revert to tried and tested methods, such as requesting copies of documents by email. This results in even greater inefficiencies and duplication of effort.

The information resources kept by a collaborative venture should be fit for purpose—and the time spent planning what is needed rather than storing everything will be well worth it.

Tips for effective communication

In order to ensure that the application of technology to collaboration adds rather than subtracts value, there are a few tips that you may wish to consider.

TAKE THE PATH OF LEAST RESISTANCE WHEREVER POSSIBLE

If universal tools such as email and telephone will enable you to fulfill the communication needs of the group, stick with them. You may well see the benefit in using a web-based discussion forum for questions and answers, for example, but if some members are not familiar with that technology, you are putting an unnecessary barrier in the way of productive discussion. Email distribution lists (sometimes known as a "listserv") with all of the relevant people included in questions and answers may achieve the same result with no need for behavioral shift or training. Do a cost–benefit analysis and choose the most cost-effective way of giving people access to information.

INVEST SUFFICIENT TIME AND ATTENTION IN COMMUNICATION AND INFORMATION-SHARING PROCESSES

Information and knowledge are the lifeblood of any collaborative venture. Many ventures have faltered as a result of poor communication. Having at least one person with responsibility for communication and information flows will significantly assist everyone else involved in the venture. As we discuss further in Chapter 9 on roles and skills, this accountability can include tasks such as:

▶ preparing updates, newsletters, and reports
▶ maintaining databases and information held on websites
▶ keeping the contacts database up to date
▶ keeping project files and records
▶ preparing information packs for new joiners
▶ moderating electronic discussions
▶ producing Frequently Asked Questions (FAQ)-type material to summarize and digest information from a range of sources.

In this world of information overload, there is tremendous value in digesting and summarizing information. For example, a weekly one-page update of principal issues, summarized from five ten-page reports, can be an enormous productivity booster for the decision makers in a collaborative venture. Of course it takes time and effort to provide this service—but it will save the time of a significant number of other players.

DOCUMENT WHAT IT IS NECESSARY TO DOCUMENT, NOT WHAT IT IS POSSIBLE TO DOCUMENT

There is no limit to what can be written down and stored in IT systems. However, writing things down takes time and should only be done when there is a clear purpose for the information. If the question "How will this information be used?" cannot easily be answered, it is probably one task to drop off the action list. Hoarding information for the sake of it can be a drain on already scarce resources. The end result is often an electronic dump of information which no one has time to sift to find the useful nuggets.

Manufacturing businesses have realized that it is more cost-effective to have just-in-time delivery of raw materials for manufacturing processes. Similarly, collaboration processes benefit from a just-in-time approach to information sharing. Rather than building up enormous reserves of information "just in case," it is far more effective to maintain the information you know is needed, and for everything else, establish processes that connect people to other people who can help. So, for example, rather than asking every working group to produce a weekly progress update for a central database that no one will consult, you might consider asking them to produce their update when the relevant stakeholders require one (perhaps for a quarterly or monthly board meeting, for example). For any other update needs, the relevant project manager can respond to an email or phone call.

One of the great opportunities in a collaborative venture is escaping some of the unnecessary bureaucracy of the parent organizations. To be productive, collaborative ventures need a strong web of communication processes, but every information-gathering process should be in response to a clear stakeholder need.

ENSURE THAT COMMUNICATION PROCESSES REACH ALL KEY STAKEHOLDERS

Depending on the focus of any particular venture, there will be different stakeholders with different information needs. A good communication strategy, documented and with assigned responsibilities, will ensure that

everyone who needs to be informed or consulted will be. Some collaborative ventures make the mistake of focusing their communication
processes on external audiences, and forget that the members of the
alliance also need to be communicated with. The fact that collaboration
is inherently a coordination process leads to a potential for communication "black holes." One partner misses an important meeting—who
briefs that person? One working group runs into issues that affect a range
of the partners, some of whom are not represented on the working
group—who makes sure all the right people are engaged to address the
issue?

The instinct of every person involved in a collaborative venture
should be to ask him or herself at every opportunity, "Who else needs to
know this?" When you are working within one organization, there is
usually a communication safety net of management briefings, project
reviews, newsletters, email and intranet communication processes, and
even fortuitous meetings by the coffee machine if you are based in the
same building. In a collaborative venture, the equivalent of this infrastructure needs to be created. Until it is in place, you run a real risk of
people being left out of the loop, which can be very damaging to
working relationships you have worked hard to establish.

KEEP THE PERSONAL TOUCH—USE THE TELEPHONE WHEN YOU CAN'T MEET

Many people working across geographic and organizational boundaries
have discovered that telephone conferencing can be a very effective way
to keep communication flows going while sustaining relationships. This
method is effective for general updates as well as supporting project discussions within working groups. Telephone conferencing enables any
number of people to connect by phone and interact with each other. It
is especially useful for smaller groups of people who know each other well
enough to recognize each other's voices. However, it can also be used
for wider communication when a shared conversation is important for a
bigger group, whether in terms of the timescale of reaching everyone, or
the importance of consistency of message.

For those unfamiliar with the approach, it is worth noting that telephone conferencing requires someone to take on a chairman or
facilitator role, effecting introductions as necessary and inviting people to
speak. Interestingly, people who have experience of videoconferencing
and telephone conferencing generally prefer telephone conferencing.
Some of this is a reflection on videoconferencing technology, which can
still have set-up difficulties or time delay/lip synch issues, has a limit to

the number of people each participant can see, and requires quite expensive technology and office facilities. Telephones, on the other hand, are accessible to everyone wherever they may be. Although there is sometimes a service charge for setting up a conference call, there are a number of providers who simply provide a phone number and PIN number, and as long as the participants call that number at the same time and provide the same PIN, they will be connected for only the cost of the phone call.

Creating an information architecture

The rather grand term "information architecture' refers to the result of a decision-making process whereby a group determines what information it needs, where it will store it, how it will be maintained, and how it will be accessed. As every collaborative venture is different, there is no single template for an information architecture. However in the box is a set of questions that it may be useful to consider.

DESIGNING AN INFORMATION ARCHITECTURE

▶ What information do we need to keep and share? Categories to consider include information:
- to meet legal requirements, for example articles of association, accounts, confidentiality agreements, and contracts
- to support the promotion and marketing of the venture, such as branding materials and an overview of venture activities
- to support the induction of new joiners, such as a collaboration charter and member profiles
- to meet the expectations of key stakeholders, such as progress reports and cost–benefit allocation agreement
- to support a communication strategy, such as press releases, newsletters, and event calendars
- to support the delivery of specific projects or initiatives, such as project initiation documents, progress reports, meeting minutes, and special interest group reference materials.

▶ How will the security and confidentiality of information be protected?

▶ How will this information be maintained to ensure that it remains current and relevant to the collaborating partners?

▶ What information and communication tools do people have available, and therefore what is the best strategy for storing and accessing this information?

▶ Who will be accountable for the information infrastructure of the collaboration, on an ongoing basis?

Information of the kind suggested above is relatively static in nature, and the aim is to have a well-organized electronic library and filing system. Other information is more dynamic in nature, and may involve using different IT tools, such as shared calendars (which assists the setting-up of meetings) or an electronic discussion forum enabling members to ask "Does anybody know...?" questions. Both static and dynamic information needs can be considered as part of the process of establishing an information architecture for the collaboration.

Once the key information needs have been determined, the second step is to determine which tools are best suited to storing and/or accessing that information. First of all, it is important to ascertain which information tools are readily available to all members of the venture. If one partner does not have Internet access, for example, this will clearly influence the approach. The purpose of a particular piece of information will dictate which information tool is most appropriate for accessing it. For example, would a newsletter be better as an email attachment (which brings it to people's attention) or stored on a shared website (which does not clog up email boxes)? Do press releases need to be publicly available on the consortium website or not? Does an electronic discussion forum need special security measures, or could a publicly available forum service be used for the sake of cost-effectiveness? Questions like these will need consideration as the information management strategy develops. All too often, information flows are treated as a by-product of collaborative working, and dealing with them is a reactive, *ad hoc* process. By taking a more strategic approach to information management and determining an information architecture in the early stages of a collaboration, significant efficiency gains can be achieved.

DEALING WITH INTELLECTUAL PROPERTY

Sharing information in a collaborative setting is often made more difficult by concerns about protecting intellectual property (IP) rights. There can be a real or imagined threat of partners "stealing" pre-existing intellectual property, for example. In Chapter 3 on Structuring, we discussed the importance of tackling this issue in the early stages of the collaboration, and the need to consider both how pre-existing IP will be treated and how new IP will be protected and shared. By discussing this issue openly in the early stages, future conflicts may be minimized or avoided altogether. As previously noted, non-disclosure agreements are useful reminders of the importance of respecting confidentiality. However, they are not a watertight guarantee. It is the experience and judgment of the participants that will determine what to share and what not to.

The importance of two-way communication

There is a regrettable tendency to think of communication as a process that gets information out to people. In fact, it is vital to remember that communication is a two-way process. Because of the challenges of stakeholder management in collaborative settings, listening is just as important as providing information. Offering people the facility to ask questions, provide feedback, comment, and amend are all important aspects of collaborative communication. A number of collaborative technology tools include facilities to add comments to documents, or poll people for their opinions or votes on particular ideas. These functions may be useful to consider, but once again, more personal methods may be required. A regular telephone conference, for example, gives people the opportunity to ask questions more easily than an email exchange. A project team or partnership board meeting may be required to ensure that complex issues are discussed and resolved, rather than expecting an electronic conversation to handle them. There is always a risk that electronic communication will be misunderstood, especially when working across cultural and language barriers. An effective communication strategy will consider content as well as process, and ensure that people can interact in a number of ways, at appropriate intervals. It is essential that there be clear accountabilities for maintaining the health and effectiveness of this communication infrastructure.

COLLABORATIVE ADVANTAGE CHECKLIST: COMMUNICATING AND SHARING INFORMATION

- Has a communication strategy been developed, covering the key communication needs of all stakeholders of the venture?
- Have accountabilities for communication been assigned to relevant individual(s)?
- Is there a need for digesting and summarizing information for the partners, for example newsletters, briefings, progress reports or FAQs? If so, who will be responsible for this?
- Is there an information architecture for the venture, covering both static and dynamic information content?
- Is there an understanding of which information and communication tools are already in use by the partners?
- Has the venture considered a range of tools to keep communication flowing, including email, telephone conferencing, and web-based tools?
- Have the partners been briefed on how to use any new technology tools, if required?
- Has a clear policy on sharing existing and/or developing new intellectual property been agreed and communicated?
- Are effective two-way communication processes in place?

8 Learning

In an ideal world, learning from experience would be considered a natural and essential part of organizational life. In practice, the time needed for review and reflection is often traded out for what are felt to be more pressing priorities. In collaborative work, because of its evolutionary nature and the range of stakeholders involved, it is essential to build learning into the fabric of the collaborative process. Of course every human being learns from experience, and every member of a collaborative process will benefit on a personal level from the learning that he or she gains. The challenge, however, is to move beyond individual learning to learning for the collaborative team, and even further, to learning for the organizations involved.

There are four spheres for learning that are useful to consider in the context of cross-organizational collaboration. These are as follows:

LEARNING SPHERES

▶ Individual learning and development for the participants in the venture.
▶ Team learning.
▶ Organizational learning, back to the parent organizations.
▶ Formal evaluation of process and outcomes.

Let us explore the challenges involved in each of these spheres.

Individual learning and development

Collaborative working is often a very stimulating experience for the individuals involved. Generally speaking, no matter what form the collaboration takes, participants will be working with people with different skills, experience, and perspectives. International collaboration will involve working with people from other cultures, and may offer interesting opportunities for travel to other countries. The specific pieces of work being undertaken by the venture may offer a range of new experiences and learning opportunities. Each person's network of contacts will be extended, which may have any number of personal and career development benefits in the longer term.

Although individual learning is not necessarily a process that can or should be "managed" from a strategic point of view, it is an important benefit of collaborative working, and may be used as one of the selling points when looking to engage individuals in the process. In the discussion about costs and benefits to participants, this should be taken into account as one of the less tangible yet important benefits that can be gained. In collaborative ventures with few financial resources, such as many in the voluntary sector, the opportunity for individuals to learn and develop is often a significant motivation—making it worthwhile for people to give their time and effort, often unpaid. Making new contacts, traveling to new places, having new experiences—all of these may have real meaning to the people involved, and should be taken into account alongside the organizational benefits.

Depending on the scope of the collaboration, it may be appropriate to actually ask the different participants what they are hoping to learn individually as a result of their participation, and where possible ensure that these learning aims are achieved.

Finally, it is worth noting that as the importance of collaborative working increases, the experience of participating in collaborative ventures will add to a person's overall market value. Learning to operate effectively in a collaborative setting is a skill that can be carried into many activities, as we explore further in the next chapter.

Team learning

If learning only happens at an individual level, many opportunities for improving the collaborative process are lost. As the group of partners works together, there will be achievements and disappointments, and much valuable experience will be gained as a result. Unfortunately learning can be ephemeral, unless it is turned into shared understanding that leads to action.

It can be extremely worthwhile to build a learning culture into a collaborative venture from the start. This may even be expressed in the collaboration charter with words to this effect:

We will take time to learn from experience, not just individually but jointly, and will use what we learn to improve the process of working together.

What does team learning look like in practice? Team learning means consciously taking time to reflect on experience, together, and ensuring that the learning gained is used for improvement. Although this may sound simple and obvious, it is frequently forgotten or dropped off the priority list, especially as the pressures of work build. Getting a collaborative group—and indeed any team—into a routine of reflecting on experience is an invaluable habit to establish.

The question of how to do this is worth a bit of thought. The US Army faced this challenge a number of years ago when, after a series of costly blunders, the senior military echelons decided to find a way of institutionalizing a learning culture rather than simply reviewing crises or mistakes after they had happened. They developed a simple but effective process known as an after action review (AAR), which is now an established part of how the US Army operates.[1] The process, which has been adopted by many other organizations, is as follows.

AFTER ACTION REVIEWS

During a collaborative activity, whether short or long term, the team invests some time reflecting on specific activities immediately after they have been completed, using these four questions to guide the discussion.

1. What was meant to happen?
2. What actually happened?
3. Why was there a difference?
4. What did we learn?

Once the discussion is concluded, the fifth question (implied but not formally included in the Army's version of the AAR) is:

5. What actions do we therefore need to take?

The power of the process is the specific sequence of questions, which helps a group "discover" what it has learnt in a structured, objective fashion.

Establishing the AAR (or a similar process) as a standard part of the group's working methods can ensure that the knowledge yield from every activity is harvested. Because knowledge and learning are intangible, it is easy for them to leak away. If you think of knowledge as a tangible product, produced at great expense by a manufacturing process, it is inconceivable that you would simply throw it away. Because you can see the physical result of a manufacturing process, you recognize the valuable asset that you have produced. In a collaborative process, one of the primary products produced is knowledge, which has the disadvantage of being invisible. Effective teams ensure that this valuable asset is kept and put to use—but this requires protected time for reflection and learning during some (or all) of the group's meetings.

There are two levels at which team learning is important in collaborative work. One level is learning that comes from the activities in which the group is engaged. So if, for example, a group of collaborating organizations has just made its first foray into a new geographical market, it would be sensible to hold a session—perhaps an AAR—to review how that process has gone and what has been learnt, in order to improve the success of the venture in that market. The second level at which learning is important is in regard to the collaborative process itself. Because difficulties are inevitable when different organizations (and individuals) work together, it is risky to allow too much time to pass before asking the questions, "How well are we working together? What can we improve?" These questions can be useful to ask at every meeting of the main collaborative group, especially if meetings are relatively infrequent. For example, if meetings are quarterly and this discussion does not take place at one of them, six months may go by before a tension or difficulty between several of the partners is addressed. Generally speaking, working process and interpersonal issues can be dealt with much more effectively if they are raised early.

Organizational learning

One of the major benefits of participating in a collaborative venture is the learning that can be gained by the participating organizations. An organization may learn a great deal about markets, technology, competitors, and many other areas as a result of working with other companies. However, having two or three people participating in an interesting collaboration is no guarantee that the organization as a whole will benefit, unless conscious effort is made to transfer some of the learning back. Again, this type of learning process is often neglected. People feel they are too busy to share with their colleagues, they may feel that their colleagues are not interested in what they have learnt (the Not Invented Here syndrome); no one takes the initiative to organize a knowledge transfer process. The end result is that one of the major benefits of collaborative working can be lost, and the participating organization (*de facto*) reduces the return on its investment.

It is relatively simple to address this issue. The individuals participating in the collaboration should consider themselves responsible for knowledge transfer back to their sponsoring organization. This can be agreed as part of their terms of reference when they join the consortium. Depending on the learning being gained from the collaboration, they should identify those departments or individual colleagues who would most benefit from some experience sharing, then make sure that it happens.

It is especially important to take responsibility for wider organizational learning when you are involved in a collaboration with organizations that are your competitors. This is one of the most effective ways of getting to know your competitors' strengths and weaknesses, and while you will be expected to respect commercial confidentiality as part of the collaborative process, it is inevitable that you will gain insights that will be useful in a competitive setting. You will undoubtedly pick up different methods of operating, innovative ideas, new approaches that your competitors may take for granted, but that add fresh ideas to the way your own organization operates.

Picking up good ideas from your competitors is one of the benefits of sometimes working in collaboration with them. However, if these remain interesting ideas planted in one person's head, then they are only marginally better than useless. Being conscious of the knowledge yield from any collaborative venture—and explicitly bringing that yield back to your own organization—is one of the ways in which you will build collaborative advantage.

The US Army, mentioned above for its innovative after action review process, did not stop at deploying that process as a mechanism for team learning. It also established the Centre for Army Lessons Learned (CALL),[2] based in Fort Leavenworth, Kansas. CALL's role is to collect and analyze a wealth of data, including the output from significant AARs, and provide related information services to their military colleagues. CALL is an example of investing in organizational learning—not just with words but with offices, staff, databases, and information services.

Knowledge transfer processes

Knowledge transfer is not as simple as it sounds. It may be useful to get the people involved in a collaboration to write up some key learning points and recommendations in a document so that the learning is recorded and made easily transferable. However, it is very likely that the most effective way to get other colleagues engaged with the lessons from the collaborative experience (of which, after all, they have not been a part) is to spend some time with them face-to-face, sharing some of the insights, but most importantly, giving them the opportunity to put these in their own context and ask questions. In companies around the world, there are hundreds of "best practice" databases, produced with much effort and often at great expense, that are gathering the electronic equivalent of dust because the authors did not appreciate this most basic fact about adult learning. If transferring knowledge and learning is truly important to the organization, it is worth investing in the kind of face-to-face interaction that produced the learning in the first place.

One aspect to learning that applies to every collaboration is learning how to collaborate. When an organization is consciously looking to build its capability to collaborate, this needs specific focus. IT outsourcing company Fujitsu Services, for example, took a pragmatic view of how best to build its collaborative capability in the early years of partnering with other organizations to deliver large IT projects. Once a particular Fujitsu Services team gained experience collaborating with a particular partner organization, the company would wherever possible put the same joint team onto the next relevant bid or project. This ensured that lessons were transferred from one collaboration to the next—without necessarily needing any lessons to be transferred to a different group of people. Some companies, on the other hand, make the mistake of using different people for every collaborative project, thus running the risk that the same mistakes will be made over and over again.

Collaborating well is a distinct skill, as we shall be exploring in more detail. It may be best to build that capability up through a smaller group of people so that a real centre of excellence is developed, before looking to extend the capability to others. In other situations it may be crucial to transfer learning from one person or team to others. The important lesson is that knowledge transfer processes should not be *ad hoc* but deliberate. Approached systematically, they will make a significant contribution to the return on investment in collaborative working.

Evaluation for learning

In this target-driven world, it is unlikely that any collaborative process will escape the requirement to measure the impact of its work and justify the investment being made by the main stakeholders. What should be measured will of course depend on the particular outcomes being worked towards. There are some general points about evaluation of collaborative work that are worth noting, as they are likely to be useful for most, if not all, collaborative ventures.

First of all, in order to build your collaborative advantage, you should evaluate the success of the collaborative process as well as actual outcomes. This mirrors the process of reviewing both projects and the working process during meetings. At the end of any collaborative process, it is worth considering what worked and what did not in terms of the collaboration itself. Ideally this process should be undertaken with all of the partners around the table, facilitated by an external person who can remain objective. As a minimum, however, each participating organization should consider the lessons learnt about the process of collaboration itself, and build those lessons into its future investments in collaboration.

It can be useful to ask the people participating in this reflection to draw a timeline of the collaborative venture, with highlights and lowlights noted. The main high and low points can then be discussed, based on the person's stories of what happened at the time, to draw out the useful points for future collaborative processes. Of course not all lessons will be transferable to other collaborations, but inevitably some of them will be. It is useful to involve the organizational sponsors as well as the people directly involved in the collaboration, as there are likely to be lessons at both levels.

Balance quantitative and qualitative measurement. Some outcomes are clearly quantifiable. If a group of companies wishes to save costs by creating a buying circle, with the aim of reducing their respective costs by, say, a minimum of 10 percent, then there is a clear quantitative measure which can be evaluated. If a group of companies decides to collaborate in order to learn more about strategic planning processes, for example, how do the participants measure whether that has been achieved? Inevitably this will be based on their subjective judgment. Therefore the best measurement system in this case is simply asking the participants what they have achieved, and whether it matches what they had hoped to achieve. If the answer is largely positive, the collaborative venture can be deemed a success. As Einstein once said, "Not everything that counts can be counted and not everything that can be counted counts."

Qualitative feedback from key stakeholders is gaining increasing acceptance as a valid evaluation measure, often expressed as personal quotes, stories, or anecdotes. Terms like "narrative-based research" or qualitative research are being heard more frequently in relation to evaluation and research processes. If one partner in a collaboration expresses the opinion that the collaborative process saved his or her organization six months of work, that is subjective, qualitative data but also entirely valid as a means of assessing the value of the collaboration. Gathering stakeholder views— however subjective—can be a useful exercise at the close of a collaborative process, and will certainly help surface more useful knowledge for the members of the collaboration.

THE STORY OF MACMILLAN CANCER RELIEF

UK-based charity Macmillan Cancer Relief chose to develop an innovative evaluation method to capture some of the less tangible benefits of a number of activities
in which it was engaged. They called this approach the "learning framework." The
charity wished to assess the impact of investments it had been making for several
years in collaborating with communities of healthcare professionals. One example
of such a community was a group of family doctors, or general practitioners as they
are known in the UK, numbering more than 80. These Macmillan GP facilitators, as
they were called, were given special funding from Macmillan to cover a half day to
a day of their time a week, over a three-year period, to devote specifically to learning about care for cancer patients and sharing that learning more widely with
fellow GP practices (which in the UK are each set up as independent businesses).
In additional to paying for their time through covering the cost of locum cover as
required, Macmillan funded several conferences a year to enable the GPs to
discuss common issues and learn more about good practices in improving the
lives of people affected by cancer. Macmillan also funded a smaller "distilling and
connecting" group of about eight GPs, known as GP Advisors, who acted as a
channel between the wider GP facilitator community and the charity.

At each of the GP community meetings and conferences, there was much
sharing of experience and generation of ideas, many of which were translated
into action when GPs returned to their practices. Some of the ideas also generated formal Macmillan programs, and ultimately, in a few cases, significant
changes in UK healthcare policy and/or practice. However, this ripple effect, this
transformation of conversations and ideas into action, is an invisible process
when looked at from an organizational point of view.

The learning framework approach was designed to make these invisible
processes visible, in order to surface the impact of processes that were quite
tangible in terms of time, money, and effort invested. The method chosen was
narrative-based, gathering stories from the members of particular groups to
explore their experience of working in this way with the charity. The documents
produced were important not so much for the written word, but for the process
of reflection and discussion that enabled their creation. Learning points arising
from the narrative gathering, which included ways in which the community support processes could be improved, were wherever possible put to immediate
use. So, for example, when it was identified that smaller groups such as the GP
Advisors benefited from discussing their working process as well as specific
tasks, this was added as a standard agenda item for their meetings.

The learning framework also helped to develop a common language about
a way of working that was still new for much of Macmillan. Working with many
people outside the organization's boundaries was a familiar process in terms
of working with fund-raising volunteers, but less familiar in terms of influencing and supporting healthcare professionals. By sharing the learning coming
from the work, other Macmillan staff not directly involved in the initial

collaborative communities had the chance to reflect on how such processes might be useful to them in their work. As a better understanding developed of the power of this way of working, the result was more organizational support for the collaborative processes that had been established.

Methodologies for assessing partnerships

As partnerships have become a more accepted way of working, different methodologies have emerged to help collaborative ventures assess their progress, in terms of both outcomes reached and the partnership process itself. There are two main types of assessment process applied:

► Evaluating to improve: Methodologies designed to be used as a discussion framework by the participants themselves, thereby helping to build better understanding and relationships. These are sometimes guided by an external facilitator.
► Evaluating to assess: Methodologies where one or more external assessors gather data, and produce feedback and recommendations. These are generally commissioned by the sponsoring or funding bodies to evaluate what they are getting in return for the investment they are making.

An example of the first type is a tool commissioned by the UK's Office of the Deputy Prime Minister, who had established a Strategic Partnership Taskforce in 2001 to help local government improve service delivery by working in partnership with others. The Taskforce asked the Nuffield Institute at the University of Leeds to develop a tool that could assist local authorities in assessing and improving their partnerships, building on their experience of doing similar work in the health and social care field. It was expressly designed as a developmental tool to undertake a rapid health check of a particular partnership and identify areas for improvement, rather than as a centrally imposed assessment method. Called the Partnership Assessment tool,[3] its key features are described in the box.

AN EXAMPLE OF A PARTNERSHIP ASSESSMENT TOOL: ASSESSING STRATEGIC PARTNERSHIP

This particular assessment tool was developed as a "health check," to enable a partnership to assess how the partnership is progressing and where improvement actions might be required. Data is gathered from all participants, using structured questionnaires covering six main aspects of partnership, and the results are discussed between the partners to determine appropriate actions.

The assessment process follows four stages:

1 Preparation

Agreeing the purpose of the assessment exercise, determining individual contributions and how the exercise will be facilitated and actioned.

2 Undertaking the assessment

Circulating briefing material, and arranging a meeting to familiarize participants with it and having them complete the various rapid partnership appraisal sheets.

3 Analysis and feedback

The facilitator analyzes the responses and arranges a feedback meeting to share, discuss and interpret the results, and agree the next steps.

4 Action planning

Taking appropriate improvement actions as agreed and/or deciding when to undertake the next health check.

The partnership appraisal questionnaires each have six statements that relate to these six key aspects of partnership:

Principle 1: Recognising and Accepting the Need for Partnership
Principle 2: Develop Clarity and Realism of Purpose
Principle 3: Ensure Commitment and Ownership
Principle 4: Develop and Maintain Trust
Principle 5: Create Clear and Robust Partnership Arrangements
Principle 6: Monitor, Measure and Learn.

The participants respond to a number of statements within each of these six headings, using a four-point semantic scale: Strongly Agree, Agree, Disagree, Strongly Disagree. The results are presented graphically using a spider diagram that clearly shows the strong and weak point of the partnership, as assessed by the participants.

Finally, the participants can give different weightings to the six principles in terms of their importance to that particular partnership. The data gathered is used as the basis for group discussion. In other words, the data is a means to an end rather than the end itself.

This tool is a good example of giving some structure to a learning process that should be a regular feature of partnership working.

The second type of evaluation process is generally one commissioned by sponsoring or funding bodies to ensure that their money is being well spent. Because of the need for objectivity, these generally involve external assessors who have not been directly involved in the partnership.

One partnership between two organizations, one based in the United States and one based in the United Kingdom, undertook a formal evaluation of the partnership every three years, to ensure that it was delivering value for both parties. The most recent evaluation involved each party commissioning an independent assessor, but the two assessors—one based in North America, one in the UK—choosing to work collaboratively to develop a common evaluation framework and approach. The sixteen questions around which they centered their assessment are described in the box.

AN INTERNATIONAL PARTNERSHIP: KEY EVALUATION OBJECTIVES AND QUESTIONS

The main evaluation objective is to assess the strategic relevance to and outcomes of the partnership for each of the partners. The specific evaluation questions to be addressed are as follows:

Strategic fit and governance

1. What are the strategic vision for, and objectives of, the partnership, and how do they fit the purpose, vision, and strategic objectives of the two organizations?
2. How does the partnership fit with the overall strategic choices in developing and maintaining partnerships within each organization?
3. What net strategic value (strategic benefit minus disbenefit) is this partnership designed to contribute to the organizations, and how does this compare with other possible modalities?
4. What are the structures and mechanisms in place for ensuring that the partnership is strategically governed? Are measures in place to track and assess whether objectives are being met?
5. Are the partnership strategic structures and mechanisms that have been adopted the best ones for achieving the stated objectives?
6. What is the level of commitment to, and ownership of, the partnership at a strategic level in the two organizations?

Partnership processes, outputs, and efficiency

7. What structures and processes exist within each institution to manage the partnership at the operational level, and how effective and efficient are they?
8. What is the level of commitment to the partnership amongst operational staff in the two organizations? Are incentive structures in place to encourage staff to collaborate across the two institutions? What costs and benefits of the partnership are perceived by operational staff of either institution?
9. What are the activities and outputs—both internal and external—of the partnership (that is, the type and number of joint activities implemented, and the immediate results in terms for example of people affected and products delivered)?
10. What is the quality of the activities and outputs?
11. What have been the costs (for example staff time, travel, internal marketing)—actual or estimated—of the partnership?

Outcomes—internal and external

12. What have been the anticipated internal (for instance, organizational improvements) and external (for instance positive change in external environments) outcomes of the partnership and its activities?
13. Have there been unanticipated outcomes of the partnership?

Overall assessment

14. What is the overall costs-benefit balance—including opportunity costs—of the partnership?
15. How could the balance be feasibly improved?
16. Could, even with these improvements, the balance be better with other partnership(s) or non-partnership modalities?[4]

Depending on the investment going into a particular partnership, there may well be merit in undertaking both forms of evaluation—the first to help the partners learn how to improve their partnership process, and the second to formally report back to key investors on the benefits being achieved by the partnership.

Taking time to learn

Learning by doing is one of the most effective means of increasing personal, team, and organizational capability. However, there can be a great divide between knowing something and actually taking action as a result.

Building in time for review and reflection, treating learning as a core business process rather than a nice-to-have option, agreeing what action is needed when lessons have been learnt—these are characteristics of a collaborative effort that intends to get the maximum value possible from its work. An important aspect of collaborative advantage is the ability to integrate learning processes seamlessly into the day-to-day activities of the venture.

COLLABORATIVE ADVANTAGE CHECKLIST: LEARNING FROM EXPERIENCE

■ Have the learning and development wishes and needs of individual participants been discussed, and where possible, met?

■ Has the personal development opportunity been used as a selling point for joining the venture?

■ Has the aim of learning from experience been articulated in the collaboration charter or equivalent?

■ Does the collaborative team have regular reviews of what is being learnt, and does it take action as a result of that learning?

■ Have the team members been taught simple processes such as after action reviews to help them with the learning process?

■ Do participants consciously transfer learning from the collaborative venture back to their parent organizations?

■ Is there a formal evaluation process for the collaboration, and does it include both qualitative and quantitative measures? Does it cover both the collaboration process and outcomes?

■ Has the process of gathering stories from stakeholders, based on their own experience and perceptions, been accepted as a valid measure for evaluation purposes?

■ Has evaluation been used as a learning process for improvement as well as an assessment process?

9 Collaborative Skills, Leadership, and Specialist Roles

It should be clear by now that collaborative working is much more of an art than a science. Moving between tasks and relationship building, balancing individual motivation with organizational agendas, building consensus, handling conflict, considering strategic issues and then nitty-gritty detail—all of this requires the skills of a consummate diplomat, an expert project manager, a visionary leader, and a marriage guidance counsellor all rolled into one. Needless to say, it is unusual to find the full range of capability in one individual. However, one of the advantages of collaborative working is that a balanced team of partners is likely to cover every major capability required.

In this chapter we explore three aspects to the people factor within collaborative ventures: skills, leadership, and roles. The first topic is a consideration of the personal characteristics that, in an ideal world, you would wish every individual participating in a collaborative venture to have, no matter what their role. The second is a reflection on leadership, focusing on the differences between leading collaborative ventures, and leading a project or line management team over which full authority is held. The differences are significant enough to warrant some attention. Third, we build up a picture of the key specialist roles that support collaborative work, and consider the skills and capabilities needed to do these well. The main specialist roles we will consider are:

▶ The organizational sponsor, who commits his or her organization to participating in a collaborative venture, and who may or may not contribute directly to the collaborative effort on a day-to-day basis.
▶ The gatekeeper or partnership manager, acting as a relationship manager between a collaborative venture and a participating organization.
▶ The partnership coordinator, providing the day-to-day support to the partnership group.

▶ The partnership facilitator, who may be either a permanent part of the collaborative team, or brought in from time to time to facilitate the working process.

▶ The project manager, ensuring that agreed tasks are implemented on behalf of all of the stakeholders. Clearly this role is not unique to collaborative working, but as with leadership, there are some unique challenges for a project manager within a collaborative setting.

Finally, as part of the consideration of specialist roles, we consider the strategic challenge of overseeing an organization's collaborative capability, and consider whether a senior role should be established to take that responsibility—something that could perhaps be described as a "chief relationship officer."

The characteristics of collaborative people

Because collaboration is built on a foundation of good working relationships and trust between individuals, the choice of individuals for a collaborative venture is a critical success factor. There are a number of qualities that come up time and time again as being important in a collaborative setting. Here is a pen picture of the ideal collaborative partner, in terms of the personal qualities of an individual.

THE PERFECT PARTNER

People who thrive in a collaborative setting tend to be:

▶ **good relationship builders**
▶ **confident without being arrogant**
▶ **tolerant of ambiguity**
▶ **flexible**
▶ **outcome focused**
▶ **interested in learning**
▶ **culturally and politically aware**
▶ **good communicators—listening as much as talking.**

These personal qualities are possibly more important considerations than subject matter expertise in many situations. Subject matter expertise can be brought in as a resource to the collaborative process, whereas these interpersonal skills are what keep the collaborative venture on the rails. To make this point even more explicit, let us look at the other side of the coin, in other words the personal characteristics that are most likely to disrupt a collaborative process.

THE NIGHTMARE PARTNER

People who disrupt or damage a collaborative process are often:

▶ **status-conscious**
▶ **arrogant**
▶ **have a strong need for structure**
▶ **uncomfortable with change**
▶ **focused on their personal agenda**
▶ **not curious about different ways of approaching things**
▶ **take a win–lose rather than a win–win approach**
▶ **poor listeners.**

Although both the perfect and nightmare partner descriptions are of course caricatures, the serious point underlying these descriptions is the need to assess the suitability of particular individuals for collaborative work. An organization may choose to enter a collaborative arrangement for all of the right strategic reasons, then destroy its chances of gaining benefit from the process by assigning the wrong individual(s) to the process.

A PERSPECTIVE FROM FUJITSU SERVICES

Fujitsu Services director Tim Gibson reflected on the personal capabilities he felt were essential to his own firm's success in partnering with others. With the increasing need to collaborate in the IT sector, generally with organizations that are competitors in other settings, he found himself knowing his counterparts in competing firms almost as well as any of his immediate colleagues. "Partnering is here to stay," he asserted, "not just a temporary fad." He believes that companies wishing to achieve collaborative advantage will need people with a special skill set, people who are outward-looking, good at relationship management, tolerant of ambiguity, flexible, pragmatic, not too status-conscious, and able to cope with the give-and-take of collaborative work. The ability to keep a positive relationship with someone who may be your partner today, your customer tomorrow, your supplier the day after, and your competitor the day after that, is a good example of the need to be flexible and comfortable with ambiguity.

The planning process for a collaboration opportunity must include an assessment of which individuals to involve. The choice should not be based simply on the person's role or who is available at the time, but on a considered assessment of whether that person has the requisite skills to make the collaborative venture work. Unfortunately, the element over which you will have little or no control is the choice other organizations make of who represents them. Nonetheless, the more skilled your representatives are, the more able they will be to deal with any less than ideal partners.

If your organization has a formal competency framework of some kind, the ability to partner well should be integrated within it. In any case, it is useful to discuss and document the characteristics you feel are essential to collaborative working, to support the decision-making processes that arise when you decide to enter into a collaboration. Your representative will be your organizational ambassador, and the wrong choice of individual can affect both the success of the collaboration and the reputation of your organization.

Collaborative leadership

The role of leadership within a collaborative structure is an essential one, as it is in any endeavor. However, as many collaborative ventures have a networked rather than a hierarchical structure, leadership is often a quality distributed across all of the participants. Everyone in a collaborative environment should feel empowered to take the lead where their skills are best suited to a task, to challenge other partners who are not playing to the agreed rules, to help motivate and encourage their colleagues. Of course, in many cases there is a nominated leader—the CEO of a joint venture company, for example, or the chairman of a consortium. Whatever the context, one of the important lessons from experience is that leadership in a collaborative setting manifests itself somewhat differently from traditional line management. It may be useful to highlight the particular leadership skills that are called upon when different organizations collaborate. These leadership qualities are described in the box.

LEADERSHIP QUALITIES FOR COLLABORATIVE WORKING

Effective leaders in collaborative settings are able to:

▶ **reconcile different views and build a consensus**
▶ **articulate and promote a shared vision**
▶ **balance the strategic and the operational**
▶ **encourage and inspire others**
▶ **hold people to their commitments**
▶ **juggle a wide range of stakeholder relationships**
▶ **deal comfortably with ambiguity and complexity.**

Managers brought up in the world of single-organization hierarchies are sometimes in for a rude shock when they first experience a collaborative environment. Yves Doz and Gary Hamel put it rather succinctly in their book *Alliance Advantage: The Art of Creating Value through Partnering*. In it they say, "Executives do not wake up one morning with an unexplained urge to collaborate. It is not in their nature."[1]

For one thing, you do not "manage" partners in the same way that you manage staff. Partners in a collaborative setting are equals, peers. The efficient process whereby disagreement can be remedied by "the boss" arbitrating is much less straightforward in a collaborative setting. Although one person may officially have the position power to impose his or her view, the reality is that the relationship with the other partners will potentially be damaged if that view is imposed, and the end result will be suboptimal. Therefore a collaborative leader needs the patience and skill to build consensus and find the win–win, even in difficult, conflict-ridden circumstances.

A PERSPECTIVE FROM MAXXIUM

Maxxium, the global brand-building partnership between four wine and spirit companies (Scottish company Edrington, owner of Famous Grouse whisky; American Fortune Brands, owner of the Jim Beam brand of bourbon; French firm Rémy Cointreau, and Swedish company V&S, owner of Absolut Vodka), has concluded that there are some very special leadership skills that make collaboration possible. Arnaud Lodeizen, Maxxium's strategy and development director, put it this way:

Our leaders have some very special qualities. They have a high capacity for listening, they don't always have to win, they understand that collaboration means give-and-take. They have to deal with complexity and make things happen in situations where it is not always clear who is responsible for what. We realized after some trial and error that these personal qualities were essential—and we now have an effective assessment process that ensures that we are hiring the right kind of people.

The need to balance the interests of a range of stakeholders can be frustrating. Action-oriented individuals who want to get on and make something happen may find it difficult to remain patient as conflicting views are reconciled. This frustration often leads to people feeling, understandably, that it would be much easier just to do something themselves, as a single organization, rather than having to bring a group of partners with them. The additional time needed to find the win–wins and build consensus is one of the costs of collaborative working. In many cases, the cost is balanced by worthwhile benefits—but in other cases it is not. Hence the importance, as we discussed in Chapter 2, of assessing whether collaboration is the best option when compared with other means of achieving something. However, with effective collaborative leaders helping to facilitate the process, the time needed to gain and keep the commitment of all partners will be minimized. With the wrong leaders in place, that consensus may never be reached at all.

As suggested above, the leadership qualities for collaborative ventures need to be understood, and leaders need to be selected against these special criteria. Collaborative leadership is not about command and control or leading from the front—it is about leading from within.

Specialist roles

As pointed out in Chapter 6 on resourcing a collaborative venture, it is often necessary to create dedicated roles whose entire purpose is the facilitation and support of the collaborative process. The idea that collaborative working is somehow devoid of any requirements for support is a misguided notion, especially since collaboration is by definition a coordination exercise. That coordination infrastructure—in terms of roles—is essential.

A number of key roles have emerged as being especially helpful. These are listed in Table 9.1 with an explanation of the unique added value that they can bring.

Table 9.1 **An overview of specialist roles**

Specialist role	Purpose	Personal profile
Organizational sponsor	To take the ultimate accountability for a specific collaboration and to ensure that the necessary resources are made available and that the organizational goals are achieved.	Appropriate level of authority. Prepared to get directly involved as needed. Acts as an ambassador for the venture within their organization.
Gatekeeper, relationship manager, partnership manager	Acts as a gatekeeper between the venture and a participant organization, always has an overview of all of the current issues and involves colleagues as needed in addressing them.	More operational than the organizational sponsor role. A doer, makes things happen. Has a good network of relationships and influence. Works closely with organizational sponsors and the partner organization(s).
Partnership coordinator	Day-to-day coordination of meetings, other events, information resources, communication processes, telephone conferences, feedback processes, etc.	Excellent planning and organizing skills. Good communication skills. Good relationship builder. Positive and cheerful.
Partnership facilitator	Can be an advisory role as well as providing facilitation of meetings and events for the partnership group, both day-to-day and/or in exceptional circumstances such as the initial goal-setting phase, conflict resolution or evaluation.	Excellent facilitation skills. Conflict resolution skills. Neutral and balanced in approach. Outcome-focused.
Project manager	Distinguished from other project managers by the requirement to balance the requirements of a wide variety of stakeholders from different organizations and still deliver.	Able to deal with ambiguity and multiple viewpoints while still delivering. Able to build a consensus out of conflicting views.

There are many issues to be considered before appointing people to such roles, such as:

▶ Which of these roles do we need for the type of venture we have?
▶ Can consortium partners provide these resources or should we bring external people in?
▶ Are they needed full time or part time, short term or long term?
▶ What capability requirements does each role have, and how can we assess people against them?
▶ How will the people we appoint be managed and paid?
▶ What will happen to them when the collaboration finishes (this should be part of the pre-agreed exit strategy)?

Some of the issues that need to be taken into account when creating such roles are captured in the stories in the boxes, from two organizations that have chosen to appoint people to dedicated partnership management roles.

THE STORY OF UNICEF

UNICEF is mandated by the United Nations General Assembly to advocate on behalf of children across the globe and to work for the protection of children's rights, ensuring their basic needs are met and increasing the opportunities they have to reach their full potential. One of the important ways in which UNICEF achieves this is through establishing strong corporate partnerships. UNICEF's New York headquarters has a department for international and corporate alliances, which focuses particularly on global alliances, and works with partnership functions in various UNICEF offices around the globe. In the United Kingdom, for example, the UNICEF Corporate Partnerships team manages relationships with about a dozen key partners, some of which have a global scope. The three key relationships, each of which has a dedicated account manager, are the following:

▶ UNICEF's alliance with British Airways on the "Change for Good" appeal, which celebrated its tenth anniversary in 2004. British Airways customers donate their unwanted foreign coins and notes during a flight, using envelopes that are placed in the seat pockets. These are then collected and the money spent on UNICEF programs around the world. Certain BA cabin crew members volunteer to be Change for Good Champions and are actively involved by UNICEF in the collection mechanism, events, and field visits.
▶ UNICEF's partnership with Manchester United Football Club, known as "United for UNICEF." The team contributes to fundraising initiatives but has also helped raise the profile of UNICEF's work, for example by a number of the players recording public service announcements about UNICEF's work.
▶ UNICEF's alliance with Starwood Hotels, known as "Check Out for Children." One dollar (or its local equivalent) is added to each guest's hotel bill as a

donation to UNICEF. Certain staff members volunteer to be Check Out for Children Ambassadors and, like the BA Champions, are linked in with UNICEF's communication processes.

A wide range of other partnerships are in place, with corporations as diverse as Ikea, EMI, Kodak, HSBC, InterContinental Hotels, and Vodafone.

UNICEF has dedicated account managers for its principal partners and shared account managers for all others. They invest in brand development for some of the joint campaigns (such as Change for Good, Check Out for Children and United for UNICEF), and have a dedicated media relations officer who works with the corporate partners to maximize the PR benefits of the collaboration.

UNICEF appreciates the importance of dedicated roles to support its partnership strategy. Hugh Yexley, manager of the Corporate Partnerships team for UNICEF UK, says:

> There is a great deal for a partnership manager to do. They find suitable projects for the money donated through the partnership, they arrange field trips for partners to visit existing projects, they produce newsletters, organize events for UNICEF champions and they work on marketing collateral. Most importantly, they are constantly looking for ways to drive the partnership forward, keep it developing.

In terms of the most important skills for a partnership manager, Hugh Yexley feels that people skills are essential, along with influencing ability, business acumen, and the ability to seek and find the win–win in every situation.

A STORY FROM THE WORLD BANK

Joan Hubbard, who works with the World Bank in Washington DC, was in a partnership management role at the World Bank Institute for seven years. Joan and three other partnership managers had responsibility for strategic partnerships that crossed national boundaries or were global in scope, and focused on knowledge exchange rather than the World Bank's traditional financial partnerships with donor agencies. In-country partnerships were managed locally.

The role of the partnership managers was to oversee key strategic alliances, and also to advise their colleagues on partnership strategies to support particular World Bank programs. They developed and published some partnership guidelines for their colleagues and also ran a number of briefings on how to manage partnerships successfully.

Joan explains how her performance as a partnership manager was judged:

> There were two sets of reviews that determined how my performance as a partnership manager was judged. One set was from my internal clients, the people I was supporting on their partnership strategy. The key criterion there was whether the partnership(s) I'd helped establish or develop had helped them to deliver or not.

> *Secondly, my direct manager reviewed my ability to develop, negotiate and conclude partnership agreements and integrate new partnerships into the programme planning process.*
>
> **Joan was an internal coach to her colleagues on the many facets of partnership working, and reflected on the range of skills required to partner effectively.**
>
> *The ability to find the common thread, find the partner's win as well as your own; being clear about what you want but also what you can give; connecting to partners as human beings and keeping your sense of humor at all times; having conversations rather than negotiations. These are all hard skills to master. I believe relationship management should be treated as a specific discipline and built into management education processes.*

The last story illustrates the fact that even with dedicated specialist roles in place, many people get involved in collaboration as part of their day job. The knowledge of how to partner successfully needs to be transferred well beyond the boundaries of specialist roles.

Appointing a chief relationship officer

So far we have considered the roles that relate specifically to a particular collaboration. However, as collaboration becomes an integral part of most organizational strategies, an interesting question arises. Should there be someone who takes a strategic overview of all of the key relationships your organization has forged?

Most large organizations will know who their strategic partners are, in other words organizations with which there is a long-term relationship or an especially significant partnership. However, they very rarely have a complete picture of the full range of collaborative relationships across the enterprise. This can lead to inefficiencies. For example, one division might build a new relationship with a different partner when it could perhaps have deepened an existing one; equally, it is not uncommon for several different divisions of a large company to build a relationship with the same partner organization in an unconnected fashion, sometimes leading the partner organization to suggest more coordination!

In recent years there has been far more awareness of the importance of intangible assets. Customer loyalty, brand awareness, intellectual capital, management capability—all of these things have come to the fore as builders of organizational value, despite the difficulty of putting quantifiable measures on them. In a connected world, the value of relationships with other organizations must also be seen as an important aspect of an organization's capability to produce value for its stakeholders. A track record of unsuccessful partnerships points to a lower estimate of the organization's capability, whereas a track record of effective collaboration would be an indicator of having achieved collaborative advantage—and the likely ability to continue to do so. If the progress of key partnerships is an indicator of either successful or unsuccessful deployment of resources, it would seem logical that these relationship assets should be mapped out, monitored, and protected, just as any other asset would be.

Although roles like partnerships manager or director of alliances are not unheard of, they are certainly not universal. Appointing someone to be the guardian of corporate relationships—at a strategic rather than an operational level—could be a valuable addition to the senior management team.

A chief relationship manager's job description might encompass responsibilities and require skills such as those listed in the box.

A CHIEF RELATIONSHIP OFFICER'S ROLE DESCRIPTION

Main responsibilities

▶ Establish a process whereby collaborative relationships meeting particular criteria (for example of a certain size, purpose, or duration) are logged in a central database and treated as organizational assets.

▶ Monitor the success of the different relationships by establishing close working relationships with the people responsible for the partnerships.

▶ Ensure that key lessons learnt from different partnering arrangements are transferred across the company as appropriate (perhaps by hosting an annual collaboration conference, for example).

▶ Identify the people in the company with experience of collaborative working, and log them in a central database.

▶ Contribute to the assessment and appointment of partnership managers and other specialist roles.

▶ For strategic partners, act as senior sponsor and relationship manager.

▶ Identify gaps in collaborative relationships and research possible partners as needed.

▶ Benchmark other companies' partnership working, including that of competitors.

▶ Develop a company-wide training program to develop collaborative working skills where needed.

▶ Act as a coach to new partnership managers.

Knowledge, skills and attitude required

▶ **Significant experience of collaborative working, for example as a partnership manager or equivalent.**

▶ **Strategic outlook.**

▶ **Broad understanding of the business and commercial acumen.**

▶ **Excellent relationship builder.**

▶ **Strong influencer and networker.**

▶ **Understanding of the legal frameworks for partnerships.**

▶ **Committed to people development.**

Although any member of the organization's senior management team may assume these responsibilities in smaller organizations, it may well be appropriate to make this type of role a full-time, senior-level role in organizations with a multitude of collaborative relationships—as either a central coordinating role, or a role positioned at major business unit level.

Making the difficult decisions

Effective collaboration is ultimately dependent on people. However good the strategic fit between organizations, however smooth the working processes, however laudable the aims, the success or failure of a collaborative venture will ultimately come down to the human beings involved. Ensuring that the right individuals are engaged in the process is a critical success factor. Ensuring that the right roles are in place to support the efforts of those chosen individuals is another significant contribution that can be made to the success of the venture. However, it will inevitably be the case that the wrong person will sometimes end up in the right collaboration. The difficult decision at that point is this: either the wrong person must be replaced or the venture will fail. It is the other side of the coin—gaining collaborative advantage means putting the right people in place, but also getting the wrong people out again once it becomes clear they do not have the necessary capability to collaborate effectively. Sometimes the issue may be personal chemistry with one or more of the other partners, sometimes it is a lack of personal capability to work collaboratively. In both situations you will have to bite the bullet—either change the person or risk failure.

COLLABORATIVE ADVANTAGE CHECKLIST: COLLABORATIVE SKILLS, LEADERSHIP AND SPECIALIST ROLES

- Have you clearly articulated the competencies required to represent your organization in a collaborative setting?
- Have you identified the key individuals who are or could be suitable for collaborative roles, with some coaching from more experienced people if required?
- Have you considered which specialist roles are required to support the collaborative venture?
- Do you have an assessment process to ensure there is a good fit between the capability of the people appointed to the specialist roles and the requirements of the roles?
- Do your leadership development processes cover the leadership challenges involved in collaborative work?
- Would your organization benefit from having one or more specific individuals taking a strategic overview of all partnership and collaborations—a "chief relationship officer"?
- Are you prepared to remove people from a collaborative process if they clearly do not have the capability to make it work?

10 Internal Collaboration

The scope of this book is explicitly defined as inter-organizational collaboration. Yet it is fairly self-evident that in order to be effective at collaborating with external partners, it is important to have the internal capability to collaborate as well. An organization rife with robber barons and strong organizational silos is unlikely to be effective at external collaboration—the culture of such an organization works against any possibility of achieving collaborative advantage.

In this chapter we therefore consider the challenges of internal collaboration, since meeting these well will go a long way towards building the capability to collaborate with outside organizations. There has been a realization over recent years that mobilizing ideas, knowledge, and expertise across a firm makes the best possible use of the intellectual capital available. Yet as companies have worked to make this happen, they have also realized that this is not as straightforward a proposition as it sounds.

In this chapter we consider:

▶ the main forms of internal collaboration and the support that they require
▶ the blockers that make internal collaboration difficult
▶ some ideas on how to overcome the most commonly encountered blockers.

The challenge of collaborating across internal boundaries

For our purposes we shall define internal collaboration as people working together across formal organizational boundaries, within one company. These boundaries may delineate functional lines, business units, or geographic operations. If someone is working with a colleague who is not part of the same official box on the organization chart, then let us consider that to be internal collaboration. Collaborating with immediate peers and team members, within a formal business unit, is of course important too, but let us consign that form of working to the well-known heading of "teamwork."

Internal collaboration is that little bit more challenging. Just as with external collaboration, you increase the chance of encountering different perspectives, motivations, and agendas for every boundary that you cross. In theory, internal collaboration is less difficult than external collaboration because within one company everyone is meant to have the same broad strategic agenda. In practice, this is rarely the case. In fact people have been known to say that it can be easier to collaborate with external partners than to collaborate with your own colleagues, because external partners sit outside the internal political battles and power games.

Let us turn to the challenges of working across internal organizational boundaries. First of all, why would you need or want to do so? The simple answer is that by working with your colleagues, you expect to achieve something quicker, more cost–effectively, or better than if you tackled it on your own. Organizational life being what it is, there is sometimes another more political reason for doing it, such as the fact that your CEO insists on it.

Lord Browne, chief executive of oil company BP, is known for having identified opportunities for synergy between a number of BP's business areas. In order to encourage the heads of these divisions to work together, Lord Browne grouped them into peer groups of about a dozen similar businesses each. Over time these peer groups went beyond simply sharing ideas, to allocating a shared investment pot between themselves and collaboratively setting targets. Lord Browne also made it clear that career progression was dependent on individuals both achieving the performance targets for their own business and supporting other businesses in BP—helping to develop what some have called "T-shaped managers."[1]

In other cases, the motivation may come from outside the company, such as a global customer demanding consistent services across a number of country operations, thus in effect forcing those country operations to collaborate in order to satisfy the requirements.

Primary forms of internal collaboration

What are some of the primary forms that internal collaboration takes? It may be helpful to look at three broad categories into which most internal collaboration efforts fall (see Table 10.1). We shall use the language of "communities," a term that is increasingly being used to describe cross-boundary groups of people, both within and across organizations.

Each of these different types of internal collaboration has its own

Table 10.1 **Principal forms of internal collaboration**

Type of collaboration	Description	Characteristics
Community of purpose	Project teams, task forces, steering groups.	A group of people held accountable for delivering an objective—for example, completing a project, winning customer business, reducing costs, deploying a good practice, completing specific research. Usually exists for a limited timescale.
Community of practice	Groups of professionals who fulfil the same role or practice, sometimes with a common reporting line to a functional head and sometimes not.	Like-minded peers who are keen to learn from each other and improve the standard of their practice. Very distinct from communities of purpose in that a CoP largely decides its own course of action and the benefits of collaborating and learning from each other emerge over time, rather than being measured on any detailed pre-set objectives. Usually a long-term process.
Community of interest	People interested in the same subject even though they may have different roles.	These groups may develop ideas about how to enter a new market or be interested in common themes such as new technology, emerging social trends or legislative developments. They are not held collectively responsible for an outcome and therefore they are not a community of purpose—and they each have different types of responsibility so they are not a community of practice. Membership often very fluid.

challenges. The universal difficulty they face is that they are part of what one might call the "invisible organization"—invisible in the sense that no organization chart reflects their existence even though tangible work is being done through these cross-boundary vehicles. All of the strategic planning, resourcing, and performance management processes of organizations tend to be built around the "official" ways of working, that is to say the business units and functions on the organization chart. When cross-boundary groups seek political support and/or resources, these can be more difficult to obtain. More commonly, these collaborative efforts are treated as an optional extra, possibly worth doing but not really part of the "day job." Their aims are often not built into individuals' personal objectives, so people get little recognition for the contributions they make to them. When it comes to allocating resources, a common experience is the outbreak of internal squabbling as to which budget(s) will carry the burden of funding the cross-boundary work. Giving internal collaboration formal support and recognition is a challenge with which many organizations are grappling.

Let us define each of the three broad categories in more detail before going on to look at the different forms of organizational support that they require.

DEFINING COMMUNITIES OF PURPOSE

Most organizations will be familiar with this form of cross-boundary working even though they might not have used the term "community of purpose." Special task forces or project teams are frequently allocated to tasks that cross business boundaries. These teams may be asked to deploy a new business process or technology, for example, or to research new market opportunities. Different organizational units supply the project team with members, and the team works together for a time to achieve a particular goal. Some form of political sponsorship leads to the group being set up in the first place, and if that support is sustained throughout the life of the project, the initiative has a good chance of success. Unfortunately, these cross-company activities are often set up without enough thought to the political support and resourcing they need, and as a result they often founder. This is another reason that organizations that are good at internal collaboration tend to be good at external collaboration—they realize that cross-cutting ventures need support and resources if they are to achieve their aims.

The key distinction of a community of purpose is that it has a clear aim and is held accountable for results.

DEFINING COMMUNITIES OF PRACTICE

There has been much interest in so-called "communities of practice" (CoPs) in recent years, as organizations have begun to realize that the best vehicle for transferring knowledge is people rather than databases. After something close to ten years of pinning hopes on information technology to mobilize intellectual capital, organizations have begun to support groups of professionals in similar roles, with knowledge-sharing processes that help each of them to improve and learn more about the work that they do, by interacting with their peers from across the company. Communities of practice typically have an organizational sponsor who gives them political support, one or more leaders who nurture them on a day-to-day basis, and often a coordinator to support them on logistical and administrative matters, depending on the size of the community. They usually have regular meetings, conferences, and workshops, as well as working groups on topical issues. They may invest in shared information resources and newsletters to keep them up to date with developments.

Some companies have found that investing in these connecting processes achieves more than just effective knowledge transfer—it builds long-term relationships between people which sustain knowledge-sharing and collaboration in between meetings, and gives the whole organization a vehicle for working through and with a wide community of people representing most, if not all, parts of the business. Those who have seen the value of this way of working have in some cases appointed full-time community leaders, which begins to give a cross-boundary group some of the benefit of being part of the formal organization while stopping short of constraining it with the full weight of business procedures and measures.

Communities of practice are very different from communities of purpose in that they generally have very broad terms of reference—such as "keeping our project management capability at world class levels"—and within those terms, the community members themselves determine what it is most important to work on. In many ways, a CoP approach is a process of supporting a group of professionals and recognizing their value to the organization, rather than directing them towards specific tasks. Traditional functions such as Finance, Human Resources and Marketing are all potential communities of practice, as well as line management structures—and some staff directors have begun to appreciate the value of meeting and sharing good ideas and useful practices as well as managing by objectives.

Other CoPs bear no relation to standard functional groups. An automotive company may have a CoP made up of all the engineers working with a particular technology for car engines; a hospital may have a CoP of all of the surgeons using laser technology; a construction company may have a CoP of all project managers. Communities of practice are sometimes "engineered," that is to say, set up by a central group that spots the need to encourage knowledge sharing in a particular community. More often than not, they simply emerge from day-to-day work, starting with a small core group who meet informally at first to share ideas, and having experienced the value of that, extend it to a more structured and inclusive process across the rest of the organization.

DEFINING COMMUNITIES OF INTEREST

Also known as special interest groups, these are cross-boundary groups that coalesce around a particular issue of interest and whose members, at least for a time, communicate with each other and share ideas and experience. Again, this may start as a very informal process, but at some point organizational support or recognition may be given if the issue is particularly relevant to the business at the time. A community of interest (CoI) does not (at least initially) have any objective for which the members are collectively accountable, unlike a community of purpose. It is more likely that the individual members each have a goal related to the topic, and the community process is helpful to them individually in reaching that goal. A community of interest is not a community of practice, in that the members may hold a wide range of different responsibilities while sharing a common interest.

A community of interest can develop into a community of purpose. For example, a CoI may identify a topic with major potential impact on the company, and out of that realization, a project group might emerge to make specific strategic recommendations. The project group becomes a community of purpose—tasked with producing a specific output and held accountable for doing so. ABN Amro Bank, for example, set up what it called "Value Area Teams," which focused on issues like sales force effectiveness and cost management, each aiming to develop some breakthrough thinking and action on its topic.

Why is it important to make these distinctions between different cross-organizational groups? There are two principal reasons.

First, unless the purpose of a cross-boundary community is made clear, there can be mismatched expectations. For example, imagine a manager is invited to a one-day company event about developments in European legislation, hosted by a few colleagues from other business units. She sees this as an opportunity to learn some useful things for her own work. Imagine her surprise if at the end of that day, she is asked to be accountable for five action points on an action plan developed at the event. She might feel under peer pressure to accept, but will soon look to unburden herself of this additional unwanted responsibility.

On the other hand, if the invitation makes it clear that an event has the purpose of producing an action plan, then the invitee can join in with the expectation that this will mean doing some work, not just picking up ideas.

Second, there are different organizational support requirements for the three major categories of cross-boundary groups. These can be summarized as follows.

SUPPORT FOR COMMUNITIES OF PURPOSE

If a cross-company team has been put together to achieve a specific objective, it will need visible support from a senior level. The reality of organizational life is that this type of cross-boundary effort will inevitably require trade-offs to be made in relation to other work. Unless the collaborative effort has strong management sponsorship, it will almost inevitably drop off the list of priorities, as more immediate management pressures are brought to bear.

One of the main reasons that internal collaborative efforts often get second priority is that the individuals involved are not specifically measured or rewarded on the contribution they make. If their performance appraisal and career development is only based on the work they do within their home unit, then it is not entirely surprising that they will put their focus there. Sponsor(s) of internal collaborative efforts often say that these are strategically important, but neglect to turn the words into action. Action would mean, for example, connecting the collaborative project to people's personal objectives and rewards.

The second unfortunate tendency is for cross-boundary teams to be given a clear objective without any additional resources to achieve it. Partly because resourcing and budget systems tend to be so oriented towards vertical silos, it can be challenging to allocate budget and resources to a group of people doing something to benefit the whole of the company or several different business units. Therefore, the resources are not found or are not released—and, not surprisingly, the internal collaboration leads nowhere as a result. Just as with external collaboration, internal collaboration needs careful thought about the resources required. If this is not done, the outcome is often great disappointment as a group of well-meaning people, initially filled with great interest and enthusiasm, find that they are unable to make the difference they had hoped to make. As we have said in relation to external collaboration, enthusiasm and goodwill can only achieve so much.

SUPPORT FOR COMMUNITIES OF PRACTICE

Until recently, most communities of practice were either formal functions such as HR, Finance, or Marketing, with budgets enabling them to meet and share ideas and good practices; or informal groups of colleagues who perhaps met on a training program and decided to keep in touch. It is only in recent years that organizations have begun to see communities of practice as a strategic tool, a way of increasing overall organizational capability and creating a channel of communication and relationships between a group of professionals which can enable them to achieve much more collectively that they would working in isolation from each other. The more recent realization is that functional professionals are not the only people who share common practices, so a community of practice could be everyone who has a project management role, for example. They might not all report to the same line manager, and yet they share a common practice.

As the value of this connected way of working has begun to be appreciated, organizations have put resources into supporting these communities—not directing them, but supporting them. Community sponsors, coordinators, administrators—the roles that are useful to supporting external collaboration are largely the same as those useful for supporting ongoing internal communities of practice. Without that support, many communities of practice wither away when the initial founding members move on. With organizational support, the community will be sustained beyond the tenure of any particular group of individuals.

The key decision for any organization is when to give that additional support and when to let the CoP continue as a volunteer-run, informal process. Both approaches can bring benefits, depending on the context and the strategic importance of that particular community's skills to the organization. As with any resourcing decision, a cost–benefit analysis should be undertaken to decide what the right balance of investment might be.

It is worth bearing in mind that some organizations have found that formalizing an informal community of practice can sometimes kill the initial enthusiasm of the participants, if they feel that their ownership of the process is being taken away. There are risks, for example, in the organization starting to assign tasks and responsibilities to a CoP. As we have said, this creates a mismatch of expectations and confuses a community of practice with a community of purpose.

As with communities of interest, it may well be that some communities of purpose emerge from a community of practice. They usually take the form of a project team or working group on a specific topic, and the contributors choose to participate, in the clear knowledge that this is not just about sharing ideas and experience, but about achieving something for the organization. These project teams and working groups will then need the support that any community of purpose needs: management sponsorship, resources to make things happen, and recognition for the work they have put in.

SUPPORT FOR COMMUNITIES OF INTEREST

Generally speaking communities of interest come and go, reflecting the shifting sands of organizational life. They tend to be initiated by one or more people with a passion for a particular topic, and through personal networks, the group expands to include a wider range of colleagues. Although it is likely that some early face-to-face meetings sparked the idea for a special interest group, this is one form of community that can often be sustained simply by offering the group some communication tools, such as email distribution lists or space on the company intranet. Just as thousands of interest groups (sometimes called user groups or newsgroups) thrive on the Internet, connecting people who have never met and enabling them to share a great deal of useful information, so an internal community of interest can share ideas without needing significant organizational support.

It is worth noting that some interest groups are largely social in nature—the company's fans of a particular sports team or the people interested in charity work, for example. Some businesses take the view that these are not directly related to the business and that therefore they should be discouraged. For example, they might not allow a social community of interest to use space on the company intranet. This can be shortsighted—the relationships that are built between people who share some personal interests will inevitably benefit their business relationships too. A colleague once quoted the example of renting a holiday home from another colleague, thanks to the "classifieds" section on their company intranet. When the person he rented from then called him months later for help with a business issue, he was very happy to help. Such low-cost company support is probably worthwhile, even if the interest is initially social rather than business-oriented.

Blockers to internal collaboration

Although there is an intuitive logic to the argument that people within one organization should pool their ideas, expertise, and knowledge in order to meet their stakeholders' expectations, the reality is that very often knowledge remains stuck, hidden away in one part of the organization even though another part might benefit from it. Despite the wide variety of organizations in the world, there is a surprisingly consistent set of reasons that colleagues do not collaborate with one another. We might summarize the issue as the organizational culture not being collaborative, but it is not until the problem is broken down to the level of individual motivation that it becomes possible to do something about it. Table 10.2 highlights the key blockers to internal collaboration, from the point of view of the individual.

The question is, how do you overcome these blockers? Leadership

Table 10.2 **Principal blockers to internal collaboration**

Blocker to internal collaboration	Explanation
Too difficult to work with others	Appears quicker to do things on your own or even to work with external partners
Don't know who to collaborate with	Not enough connecting between business units for people to know what others are doing
"Not invented here" syndrome	People can be suspicious of other people's motivation for proposing collaboration and often don't support something that wasn't their idea to begin with
"Knowledge is power" syndrome	Concern that collaborating with others somehow decreases someone's unique value to the company
Unwilling to ask for help	Concern that asking for help shows weakness
Accountability issues	Who will get the credit if it works or the blame if it goes wrong?
Cutting across the organizational structure	Difficulty positioning the collaborative effort in the power structure of the organization and/or ensuring it gets the resources it needs

plays a key role, as overcoming these blockers does mean shaping the whole working environment to encourage collaboration. We now look at a range of practical actions that help to address some of these blockers.

Encouraging and rewarding internal collaboration

As we have said, an organization's culture is the context within which cross-boundary communities develop. If the culture is naturally collaborative, this will be an easy step. If, on the other hand, the culture is internally competitive, with well-defended internal boundaries, shifting to a more collaborative way of working is a major business transformation, not simply the introduction of new processes to connect people. It is important—in fact essential—for leaders to reinforce the value of collaborative working, by encouraging and rewarding people for working with and learning from their colleagues.

What does this encouragement and reward look like in practice? A number of stories and examples follow.

THE STORY OF PEARSON

International media group Pearson, whose major businesses include Pearson Education, the Financial Times Group, and the Penguin Group, developed an innovative approach when chief executive Marjorie Scardino, having successfully rationalized and focused the business portfolio, identified the need and opportunity for more working across the businesses within the Pearson Group. In 2002, the Pearson leadership team decided that a specific focus on internal collaboration was important to help make the boundaries between Pearson businesses more permeable, more open to each other's ideas, expertise, and innovations. As a catalyst for change, they therefore established a "collaboration bonus" for the top 100 Pearson managers, designed as one part of their financial incentive package.

Each manager identified an opportunity to work with another Pearson business unit on a specific business initiative, and agreed with his or her chief executive that this particular business target would be the one measured for the collaboration bonus. At the end of the year, the chief executive reviewed the results of the collaboration and the relevant bonus was allocated, having been vetted by a senior HR person to ensure consistency and fairness across the different businesses.

In the first year of the collaboration bonus scheme, a Collaboration Prize was also established, which awarded $50,000 to the joint teams that had achieved the most through collaborative working. Different businesses submitted their nominees for the collaboration prize, and a senior director reviewed the nominated projects and awarded the prize to the project that best met the company's criteria. This well-publicized award added to the awareness of the strategic importance of internal collaboration.

As well as awarding the Collaboration Prize, Pearson kept the collaboration bonus in place for two years to act as a longer-term stimulus for change. By linking it to the company's performance management system, it sent a clear signal to the senior management community that internal collaboration was not just a "flavor of the month" set of words but an important aspect of how Pearson expected to create value from its portfolio of businesses.

In 2004, with two years of internal collaboration experience under their belt, it was felt that enough business value had been demonstrated and experienced that it was not necessary to maintain a separate collaboration bonus. Internal collaboration was becoming, as it should, a natural part of "how we do things around here."

In addition to the collaboration bonus and prize, Pearson established a number of communities of practice called "forums." The first forums emerged around Design, Marketing, People, and IT. These were initially supported centrally with a budget and resources. Over time, the different communities were expected to take full ownership of their processes, if and when they felt there was value in meeting and sharing ideas. Pearson's management development director Alison Young commented:

> Forums are a very useful mechanism for building strong personal networks across the business. They help people feel connected to the bigger business and also make them feel valued and appreciated. But they should only be sustained if people feel they are worth it—otherwise the energy just fizzles out.

The Pearson example is an interesting case of a situation that lies somewhere between internal and external collaboration. The companies concerned were all part of the same group, yet were distinct legal entities, with their own culture, business processes, and market focus. The major difference is that because the companies are part of the same governance structure, it is possible to take leadership action to foster more collaboration. National governments, to some degree, have the same possibility open to them—with enough political will from the top, collaboration between different government departments can be strongly encouraged (if not mandated).

OVERCOMING THE CLASH WITH THE FORMAL ORGANIZATION

Any cross-boundary group, whether permanent or temporary, can be perceived as a threat to the formal organizational structure. If the internal collaboration has strong senior management support, it may be

resented—and possibly undermined—by people not invited to participate. If the internal collaboration does not have strong support, it will
probably be ignored. Depending on the scope of the collaborative effort,
it may be competing for scarce resources, and run into opposition from
established units for that reason.

The more hierarchical the organization, the more a networked, collaborative approach can sit uneasily with the power dynamics of the
organization. The public sector generally has well-established hierarchies, and this can present a particular challenge when government
departments seek to work in a more "joined-up" way. As Stephen
Goldsmith and William Eggers point out in their book *Governing by
Network: The New Shape of the Public Sector*,[2]

> *government's organizational, management and personnel systems
> were designed to operate within a hierarchical, not a networked model
> of government, and the two approaches often clash.*

The clash with formal organizational processes should not be underestimated
as a blocker to collaborative working. The box has an example.

A STORY ABOUT SETTING UP A COMMUNITY OF PRACTICE

A large government department in the United Kingdom had identified approximately 80 specialists in a particular domain who, they believed, would benefit from being supported as a community of practice. These specialists had an
important public-facing role, and the consistency and quality of the service
they offered depended on each of them keeping up to date with the latest
developments in the field. Within the formal organization structure, the
specialists reported in to a range of different offices across the country. A
policy coordinator in the department's central office took on the coordination
role, engaged several of the specialists in a small steering group, and worked
with them to design a community of practice approach that their colleagues
would value. Knowing the importance placed on hierarchical position, he
made sure that the specialists' line managers were all informed of the inten-
tion to build the connections between this group of specialists. Without the
managers' support, the individuals would not be able to travel to meetings or
conferences of the community.

All seemed to be in place to create a new collaborative process for a
valued group of professionals. A kick-off conference was planned to which all
were to be invited. Because this event would involve about 80 people, and be

a residential event over two days, the cost was not insignificant. And this is where a common pitfall was encountered: how would this event be funded? The policy coordinator had no budget for such events; the specialists could cover their own travel expenses with their manager's support but not the cost of the event itself; there was no process within the financial system for splitting the cost across 50-plus cost centres. Although the total amount of money was minuscule compared with the overall budget of the department, the issue ended up being discussed at board level before it was resolved, by reallocating budget to the central coordinator to pay for the event.

The ability to resource cross-boundary work is an essential development needed for most organizations' formal budgeting processes. As with any innovation, the key is not to be constrained by "how we've always done things around here." The chief executive of a large local authority in the United Kingdom developed an innovative solution when he discovered that his own organization had no mechanism to fund work that spanned the boundaries of different organizational units. Realizing that changing the accounting processes would be a time-consuming task, he set up what he dubbed "the Chief Executive's Hospitality Fund," within his own cost centre for the Chief Executive's Office. Any group within his authority that identified a need for people to work across boundaries—in other words, that was interested in setting up a community of purpose, practice, or interest—could apply for budget from his fund. He reserved the right to refuse if he felt the project did not deliver enough benefit, but created a mechanism that offered real speed and flexibility to the organization when cross-cutting issues arose. It is this kind of creativity that is needed to shift from processes that are rooted in the past to processes that support the actual requirements of today's organizations.

OVERCOMING THE "NOT INVENTED HERE" SYNDROME

The so-called not invented here (NIH) syndrome tends to manifest itself when a part of the organization offers to share something it has learnt with other parts of the organization—for example, in the context of a best practice sharing initiative. This is an ideal opportunity for effective internal collaboration, an opportunity to ensure that 1 + 1 = 3 and to reuse knowledge rather than reinvent wheels. Unfortunately, many such efforts fail to achieve any significant impact, in part because of the lack of understanding of the NIH syndrome. If people feel that some other group's ideas and experience are being imposed upon them, with no understanding of their pressures or their business context, rebellion—or even worse, paying lip service to the initiative—is a likely outcome.

There are a number of possible steps that can be taken to minimize the impact of the NIH syndrome. The first is to choose appropriate language to describe what you are trying to do. Anything referred to as a "best practice" builds in instant confrontation, as it begs the question "best for whom?," implies by definition that the recipient has "worse" practices, and suggests that someone else has the authority to judge what is "best" for the recipient. Refer to these practices as good practices, interesting practices, valuable practices, useful ideas, tips and hints—any of these labels avoid the automatic implied insult of the term "best practice."

A metaphor that has been found to be helpful is that of "recipes." If an organization has found an effective way of doing something, it could be said that it has found an effective recipe for something. If you were to offer a cookbook full of useful recipes to someone, they would generally not feel offended or look for ways of rejecting the gift. Why not? Because they are in control of which recipes they choose, they can modify the recipes to suit their individual preferences and circumstances, and the recipes save them time without limiting their creativity. That sense of control, the notion that you may have useful experience yourself which can improve the recipe—all of this helps human beings to welcome ideas from elsewhere. So the first step is to use a label and style that reflects all of the positives of a "cookbook" approach.

Second, the process that is designed to share the good practice is often approached as a "telling" exercise rather than a learning exercise. If you want to tell someone about a good practice, you can present it to him or her or write it down in a document. If you are lucky, you may transmit some information using these means, but it is very unlikely that you will engage your colleague in doing something differently. One of the most common mistakes is to focus on documenting so-called "best practices" and putting them in a database for others to use. The argument for this approach is often that it appears to be the most efficient and cost-effective way of spreading best practices quickly. Unfortunately it often proves to be a complete waste of time and effort.

To illustrate this point, let us consider the example of a "lessons learnt" process implemented by one of the UK's military services. Similar to the after action reviews implemented by the US Army, this service had an effective process to capture lessons from the service's significant activities, and these were documented in a Lessons Learnt database. At one point a review was undertaken of all of the lessons documented in the database, whereupon the service realized that many similar mistakes were still being made. As a senior officer put it, the organization realized it had a "lessons documented" process, not a "lessons learnt" process. The simple step then taken was to ensure that, at any lessons learnt review, people were made accountable for implementing any actions required, such as changes to policy, procedures, or training. Unless databases are connected in some measurable way to action, they usually fill up with interesting documentation that no one reads or uses.

Sharing good practices usually works best in face-to-face encounters. This is a learning process, which should be centered on the needs of learners rather than what someone wants to tell them. Oil company BP is well known for a process it calls a "Peer Assist," which connects people with experience to people who want to know more. The important point is that the request comes from the people who want to know, thus starting with an incentive to learn rather than starting with a desire to transmit something to someone who may or may not be receptive.

OVERCOMING THE "KNOWLEDGE IS POWER" SYNDROME

There is a commonly held perception that people resist collaborating with their colleagues because "knowledge is power," and by cooperating with others, they will somehow be losing that power. This might have been true in a world where access to knowledge and information was restricted. In today's information-rich environment, people are generally drowning in knowledge and information rather than struggling to find it. However, it is undeniable that people generally do not share knowledge and collaborate with others unless there is something in it for them. Therefore, the "What's in it for me?" (WIIFM) syndrome is probably a more accurate description of this issue, in terms of the challenge of unlocking each individual's desire to collaborate with others. It is almost always possible to find a "WIIFM" — recognition, visibility, a free lunch, even simply a sincere thank you.

OVERCOMING THE UNWILLINGNESS TO ASK FOR HELP

Document company Xerox used a self-assessment tool whereby different business units assessed their capability in relation to a number of practices that were seen to be of strategic importance to the company. The results were then made public, and each unit could see its results relative to other units. It was then up to the unit to contact those that had given themselves higher ratings if it wanted to improve this particular area in its business. Choice, self-assessment rather than people sitting in judgment—these are approaches much more likely to gain people's commitment, interest, and willingness to ask for help from their colleagues. Having a structured process in which everyone participates also removes the stigma of asking for help.

THE STORY OF GENERAL ELECTRIC

An example of generating motivation to work across boundaries came from American conglomerate General Electric (GE), from the days when Jack Welch was in charge. He had made it clear that the sharing of good ideas across boundaries was one of senior management's top responsibilities. This posed a particular challenge for GE managers because of the size and diversity of the businesses in GE. If you did have a good business idea, how could you identify the people in other businesses who might benefit from it?

The chief learning officer at GE at the time came up with a simple solution. He put in place a "hot line" telephone number manned by his team, who acted as a sort of dating agency, to match good business ideas with business units that might benefit from their colleagues' experience. This took much of the burden away from the line managers, who could then concentrate on running their own businesses while ensuring that good ideas did move across business boundaries. As a result of the expectations from the top, clearly communicated and reinforced by Jack Welch, and some simple support processes, GE overcame much of the natural inertia that keeps good practices trapped in one part of an organization.

The importance of building internal collaborative advantage

Creating effective connections across formal business units within one company means facing many of the same challenges as external collaboration. In fact, in large organizations made up of diverse businesses, the whole experience is very akin to external collaboration. There are the same challenges of developing a shared agenda, motivating people to participate, working across different cultures, and supporting the collaborative effort with appropriate roles and resources. For this reason, involving people in internal collaborative ventures is excellent preparation for getting them involved with external collaboration.

It is very unlikely that an organization with an adversarial, hierarchical, internally competitive culture will have the capability to build collaborative advantage in its marketplace. In this aspect of organizational life, as with so many others, charity (so to speak) must start at home.

COLLABORATIVE ADVANTAGE CHECKLIST: INTERNAL COLLABORATION

- Is there a common language and understanding about different forms of internal collaboration, such as communities of purpose, practice, and interest?
- Do budgeting and resourcing processes include the facility for resourcing cross-boundary work?
- Are there recognized roles and responsibilities for supporting cross-company work?
- Do senior leaders make their expectations for cross-boundary working clear?
- Are people recognized and rewarded for collaborating internally?
- Have creative solutions been found to the major blockers to internal collaboration, focusing on the "WIIFM" (What's in it for me)?
- Is internal collaboration used as an opportunity to build the skills for external collaboration?

11 Developing Collaborative Capacity

Now we have explored the different facets of collaborative working, there is one overarching challenge that remains to be addressed. How can an organization develop its capability to collaborate effectively with others? Knowing what needs to be done is one thing; having the individual and organizational capability to do it well is another.

In this context, individual capability may be defined as a person having the knowledge, skills, and attitude to achieve particular collaborative outcomes successfully. Organizational capability may be defined as having the organizational culture and processes to support collaborative working. There are a number of aspects to building collaborative capability in both the individual and organizational domains. Let us look at each of these in turn.

Developing individual capability

In order to have the capability to build collaborative advantage, a number of people within your organization will need to have relevant knowledge, skills, and attitudes. Broadly speaking, there are three main categories of people who need to contribute to collaborative working. These are:

▶ the people who give collaboration political support within the organization
▶ the people who represent the organization in collaborative ventures, at a strategic level
▶ the people who support collaborative working at an operational level.

A summary of the individual capability required for each type of role is given in Table 11.1.

The number of people who need to have these capabilities will of course depend on the size of the organization and the number of collaborative ventures with which it is involved, or expects to be involved. If you wish to ensure that the required level of capability is in place, what are the approaches that you might consider? Some suggestions follow.

159

Table 11.1 **Developing individual capability**

Who?	Knowledge	Skills	Attitude
Senior leaders, sponsors	Shared understanding of the strategic importance of collaborative working.	Ability to successfully sponsor and support collaborative work within the organization.	Respect for partners, treating collaborative relationships as important assets.
People directly involved in collaboration, at a strategic level	Shared understanding of the strategic importance of collaborative working and the practical actions to make it work.	Relationship building. Project management. Conflict resolution. Stakeholder management.	Ambassador for the collaborative effort within and beyond the organization. Flexible, adaptable. Tolerant of ambiguity.
People supporting the collaborative process at an operational level	Clear on the desired outcomes for the collaborative venture. Good personal relationships with the key stakeholders.	Planning and organizing. Project management. Stakeholder management.	Sensitive to the needs of different stakeholders.

COMPLETING A SKILLS AUDIT

It may be that you have more collaborative capacity than you think. People who work for your organization may have been involved in collaborative ventures at other times in their professional career, or in their non-professional life. Finding out who has collaborative experience may be a useful step if you do not have that information available today. This may simply be a case of adding this aspect to an existing skills database or competency framework—or it may be a special exercise that you undertake in order to identify people who could contribute to collaborative ventures.

ASSESSMENT PROCESS FOR COLLABORATIVE ROLES

If you conclude after some form of skills audit that your people have relatively little experience of collaborative working, there is the option of assessing people for their inherent capability to work in this way. Having agreed the key capabilities required—some suggestions are outlined in Chapter 9—and either designed an assessment process to test them or used existing data such as performance reviews and/or feedback from colleagues and managers, you should then be in a better position to appoint the right people to collaborative roles.

MAKE VERSUS BUY

If there is an urgent need to increase capability in this skill area, and the organization has little experience to date, it may be that the most efficient option is to recruit people with significant experience of collaborative working. The risk factor is that they will need time to become integrated into your own organization's ways of working, but recruitment is potentially a rapid means of increasing capability. For organizations in the private or public sector, it is worth remembering that the voluntary sector has outstanding skills in influencing people, and working collaboratively tends to be second nature. The voluntary sector is a possible source of skills which is often overlooked.

MENTORING AND COACHING

Learning from experience is often the most effective way of transferring knowledge. If you have experienced people working in collaborative ventures, you might consider putting less experienced people to work alongside them, in order to develop their skills. In addition, you might consider continuing a mentoring or coaching relationship between more experienced and less experienced individuals, so that the less experienced individuals have someone they can call upon for help and advice while they are still new to collaborative working.

TEAM-BASED LEARNING

Most collaborative ventures will involve a number of players from your organization, some in leadership roles, some in support roles. In the early stages of developing your collaborative capability, you might consider moving the same team (or at least the same core set of people) from one partnership to the next, thereby developing in-depth relationships between them as well as developing their collaborative working experience. The working relationships and trust that build up over time may give you a better result than spreading the experience over a greater number of people, each working on a smaller number of ventures.

MANAGEMENT EDUCATION

If your organization does see collaborative working as an important part of business strategy, a common language and shared understanding of what this means needs to be built into existing management education processes. Management education should ideally cover all or most of the aspects of collaborative working discussed in previous chapters—both strategic and operational. An overview of your organization's most important existing relationships could also be integrated into this educational process.

CUSTOMIZED SKILLS TRAINING

As well as general management education, focused skills training to prepare people for collaborative working can be a useful investment, depending on the number of people who need capability in this area. You may wish to consider a "just in time" approach where people about to embark on a collaborative venture are given this training, tailored to the particular characteristics of the venture they will be embarking upon. You might like to use some of your more experienced practitioners as contributors to this kind of workshop.

EXPERIENCE SHARING WITH OTHER ORGANIZATIONS

As collaborative working becomes an increasingly important feature of organizational life, educational and experience-sharing processes, though still hard to find, are beginning to develop. For example, in the field of higher education in the United States, an organization called the Association for Consortium Leadership (ACL)[1] was set up to give guidance and support to higher educational institutions looking to develop cooperative programs. Now with 65 higher education consortia members from across the country, ACL provides a range of services to its members, including a mentoring program for institutions new to cooperative working, a national directory of consortium programs in higher education, and an annual conference which gives members the opportunity to share ideas and experience.

The National Council for Voluntary Organisations in the United Kingdom set up a collaborative working unit in 2004 to advise voluntary and community organizations on achieving savings and improving services by working more closely together. The advice given covers approaches such as shared delivery of projects, and developing shared services such as resources and payroll functions. The unit, run by three staff, promotes joint working among charities that have yet to consider such a move.

Collaborative working requires a particular set of personal competencies, and there is an increasing knowledge base available about what works and what does not. A conscious strategy to develop these competencies will help you to avoid some of the more common pitfalls, and build collaborative advantage more quickly and effectively.

Building organizational capability

As we have said, organizational collaboration always takes place at two levels—the relationship between individual people and the relationship between organizations. Building collaborative capability also takes place at two levels, and the second of these is the organizational level. The shift required at an organizational level can be described as outlined below.

Table 11.2 **Developing organizational capability**

Capability	Shift required
Business processes	*Strategic planning:* treat collaboration as a strategic option in core decision-making processes.
	Resourcing: ability to resource cross-boundary work, internally and externally.
	Performance management: recognize and reward collaborative working within the formal and informal performance management system.
Organizational competencies	Articulate the competencies needed for collaborative working and assess against them as required.
	Identify people with experience of or aptitude for collaborative work.
Organizational culture	Encourage openness, flexibility, teamwork, cultural awareness, respect for other viewpoints.

We will now look at these three facets in more detail.

Integrating collaborative advantage into business processes

STRATEGIC PLANNING

As discussed in some detail in the early chapters of this book, collaborative capability means considering the possibility of collaboration as one facet of a strategic decision-making process. Different organizations will of course have different strategic decision-making processes, with varying degrees of formality. However, it is important to consider the possibility of collaboration, as one of the automatic questions asked, whether this is done through informal conversation or formal, documented processes.

The individuals involved in strategic planning need to add a new perspective to their professional approach, namely the ability to analyze what has been called "collective competition"[2] and to determine the best web of alliances for their particular organization, bearing in mind the web of alliances of their competitors.

RESOURCING

We have already identified the difficulty that most resourcing processes are set up to serve a particular business unit or function. Resourcing something that cuts across organizational boundaries, whether those boundaries are internal or external, tends to be difficult and time-consuming. There is no one way of removing this obstacle, and creativity is often required, especially when you are looking to pool resources from a range of different organizations. What is important within your own organization is the facility to enable internal and external collaborative efforts to be resourced without months of internal wrangling and bureaucracy. Testing your resourcing processes on one or two pilot cases of collaborative working should be sufficient to identify the glitches in the system and enable you to iron them out.

PERFORMANCE MANAGEMENT

A further link to business process is the ability to recognize and reward collaborative working within the organization's performance management system. It is important to ensure that collaborative work is registered in people's personal objectives and linked to formal reward as appropriate. This eliminates the common perception that collaborative working is somehow not part of the "day job."

Organizational competencies

If the skills of collaborative working are recognized within the formal competency framework of an organization, it gives managers the opportunity to both invest in the development of these skills and use them as a reason to further someone's career.

As an example, the UK's National Health Service developed a leadership framework which included this particular leadership quality.

COLLABORATIVE WORKING: THE NHS LEADERSHIP FRAMEWORK

Collaborative working

Being committed to working and engaging constructively with internal and external stakeholders.

Why it matters

Collaborative working is critical in delivering measurable and radical health improvements in a complex and changing health and social care environment. Effective partnership promotes the sharing of information and appropriate prioritisation of limited resources. It also supports "joined up" provision of integrated care. The quality of dialogue in collaborative working is critical so that problems can be identified and common solutions agreed. Partners or "stakeholders" include patients, carers, health service staff and people working in other statutory or voluntary agencies. Being committed to working and engaging constructively with internal and external stakeholders

Forges partnerships for the long term

▶ **Maintains positive expectations of other stakeholders, even when provoked, and strives to create the conditions for successful partnership working in the long term.**

▶ **Is informed on the current priorities of partners and responds appropriately to changes in their status or circumstances.**

▶ **Ensures that the strategy for health improvements is developed in a cohesive and "joined up" manner.[3]**

Formally articulating collaborative capability as part of a competency framework is one way of integrating it into the fabric of the organization, making it part of "how we do things around here." Smaller organizations may not have a formal framework of this kind, in which case discussing the qualities needed and making them explicit can be done in less formal ways. As we have previously covered, clearly articulated competencies can also be used as the foundation for assessment processes that aim to appoint the right people to collaborative roles.

Influencing organizational culture

It can be very difficult for individuals to engage successfully with other organizations if their own organization has a working environment that goes against many of the principles of collaborative working. Some of the indicators of cultural incompatibility with collaborative working include:

▶ strong hierarchical structure
▶ "need to know" culture
▶ status-conscious managers
▶ inward-looking
▶ internally competitive
▶ resistant to change.

It may be extreme to suggest that the organization's culture must be changed before achieving collaborative advantage is possible, but there is some truth to this assertion. In practice, the cultural shift can happen one step at a time, taking care, for example, to put the right people in place on any specific venture and to give the collaboration enough space so that it is protected from the wider organizational culture. Other tactical steps may be appropriate, such as moving the venture into physical premises away from the "incompatible" parent organization, and where possible setting up a separate entity, which can then develop its own culture and values.

With strong political sponsorship as a form of protection, it may be possible to undertake an effective collaboration despite an organizational culture that works against it. However, it will require even more energy and persistence to see it through to a successful outcome.

The value of change agents

If you have identified a need to build greater collaborative capability in your own organization, you will, by definition, need a strategy to do so. In a world where initiative overload is a common complaint, having a "collaboration initiative" will only stimulate the organizational antibodies to new initiatives. However, as we have seen, there are many facets to building collaborative capability. There are people to be educated and trained, processes to be modified, cultural shifts to be made. If developing collaborative advantage is a strategic imperative, it is unlikely that the right elements will be put in place without some focused attention, at least for a time.

If there is a senior person responsible for overseeing major collaborative relationships across the organization, there is a natural home for the organizational development work that can support this process. It might, for example, be useful to support that individual with a small team of change agents (internal and/or external) who take responsibility for the principal actions that will develop the organization's collaborative capability. This small team could work with business process owners, line managers, HR professionals, and others to identify the opportunities to integrate collaborative approaches into the company's way of working. The philosophy should be one of integration with existing processes and ways of working rather than a new and separate initiative. A small catalyst team could also act as a learning vehicle, ensuring that lessons learnt in one collaborative venture are transferred to others, and supporting the people involved in collaborative work as a community of practice.

If there is no clear home for the business transformation work required, perhaps a cross-functional team with top-level sponsorship could act as the change agents for a period of time. It could act as a kind of collaboration conscience, making sure that the value of collaboration is understood and applied where appropriate. When collaborating with others has become second nature, it will no longer be necessary to have these dedicated change agents. However, it would be unrealistic to expect to increase collaborative capability without some focused effort for a time.

A new management philosophy

However skilled a group of change agents might be, it can only achieve results with full and visible backing from the senior leaders of the organization. Collaborative advantage is achieved as a result of a management philosophy. The leaders of the organization need to ask themselves:

▶ Are we committed to opening up to partner organizations?
▶ Are we ready to invest for the long term in these relationships?
▶ Are we prepared to accept the give and take of collaboration?
▶ Are we prepared to give the people who represent us in collaborative ventures the support and investment that they will need?
▶ Are we prepared to invest in developing our own collaborative capability?

If the answer is yes to all five questions, the foundation for success is laid. Achieving collaborative advantage will then be a continuing challenge—as the cliché goes, a journey rather than a destination—but a world full of possibilities will open up. For any skill your organization lacks, find a partner that has it. For any market you have not mastered, find a partner who has. For any subject you have not yet fully understood, work with organizations that have. Once you have embraced a collaborative philosophy, and developed your collaborative capability, the only limit to what your organization can achieve is your collective imagination.

Notes

Chapter 1

1 See for example Dyers (2000).
2 For more detail see for example Doz and Hamel (1998), chapter 1.
3 See www.scotch-whisky.org.uk.
4 See www.elfaa.com.
5 See www.cotton.org.

Chapter 2

1 See www.starck.puma.com.
2 From press release on www.honda.com website.
3 From press release on www.honda.com website.
4 From website of the Cambridge Network,
   www.cambridgenetwork.co.uk.
5 Collison and Parcell (2004).

Chapter 3

1 Axelrod (1984).
2 From the Fujitsu Services home page, www.fujitsu.com.
3 Quote from Paul Hermelin, CEO, on Capgemini's website,
   www.capgemini.com.
4 Microsoft (2002).

Chapter 4

1 See www.globalknowledge.org. Used with permission.

Chapter 5

1 Collins (1999).
2 Based on a model originally put forward by Bruce Tuckman in 1965.

3 See for example Hampden-Turner and Trompenaars (1997) or Lewis
   (2000).

Chapter 6

1 See www.crc.gov.au.
2 See www.crca.asn.au.

Chapter 7

1 Author interview with Peter Hewkin, managing director of the
   Cambridge Network.

Chapter 8

1 For more detail see Sullivan and Harper (1996).
2 See www.call.army.mil.
3 Office of the Deputy Prime Minister (2003). This Crown copyright
   material can be downloaded from www.odpm.gov.uk/ssdp.
4 Source: from working papers. Used with permission.

Chapter 9

1 Doz and Hamel (1998), p. 225.

Chapter 10

1 Hansen and von Oetinger (2001).
2 Goldsmith and Eggers (2004), p. 22.

Chapter 11

1 See www.acl.odu.edu.
2 See, for example, Casseres (1996).
3 Excerpt from the NHS Leadership Qualities Framework as published on
   www.executive.modern.nhs.uk.

References

Axelrod, Robert (1984) *The Evolution of Cooperation*, New York: Basic Books.

Balloch, Susan and Taylor, Marilyn (eds) (2001) *Partnership Working: Policy and Practice*, Bristol: Policy Press.

Casseres, Benjamin Gomes (1996) *The Alliance Revolution*, Boston, Mass.: Harvard University Press.

Child, John and Faulkner, David (1998) *Strategies of Co-operation: Managing Alliances, Networks and Joint Ventures*, Oxford: Oxford University Press.

Collins, Jim (1999) "And the walls came tumbling down," in F. Hesselbein, M. Goldsmith, and I. Somerville (eds), *Leading Beyond the Walls*, San Francisco: Jossey-Bass. pp. 24–5.

Collison, Chris and Parcell, Geoff (2004) *Learning to Fly: Practical Knowledge Management from Leading and Learning Organizations*, London: Wiley.

Doz, Yves and Hamel, Gary (1998) *Alliance Advantage: The Art of Creating Value through Partnering*, Boston, Mass.: Harvard Business School Press.

Dyers, Jeffrey (2000) *Collaborative Advantage: Winning Through Extended Enterprise Supplier Networks*, New York: Oxford University Press.

Goldsmith, Stephen and Eggers, William (2004) *Governing by Network: The New Shape of the Public Sector*, Washington, DC: Brookings Institution Press. p. 22.

Hampden-Turner, Charles and Trompenaars, Fons (1997) *Riding the Waves of Culture: Understanding Diversity in Global Business*, New York: McGraw-Hill.

Hansen, Morten T. and von Oetinger, Bolko (2001) "Introducing T-shaped managers: knowledge management's next generation," *Harvard Business Review*, March 2001.

Huxham, Chris (ed) (1996) *Creating Collaborative Advantage*, London: Sage Publications.

Leathard, Audrey (ed) (2003) *Interprofessional Collaboration: From Policy to Practice in Health and Social Care*, Hove: Brunner-Routledge.

Lewis, Jordan (1995) *The Connected Corporation*, New York: Free Press.

Lewis, Richard (2000) *When Cultures Collide*, London: Nicholas Brealey.

Microsoft (2002) *Microsoft Computer Dictionary*, 5th edition, Microsoft Press.

Office of the Deputy Prime Minister (2003) *Assessing Strategic Partnerships, Partnership Assessment Tool.* Crown coyright. Can be downloaded from www.odpm.gov.uk/ssdp.

Sullivan, Gordon R. and Harper, Michael V. (1996) *Hope is Not a Method,* New York: Times Business/Random House.

Sullivan, Helen and Skelcher, Chris (2002) *Working Across Boundaries: Collaboration in Public Services,* Basingstoke: Palgrave Macmillan.

Surowiecki, James (2004) *The Wisdom of Crowds: Why the Many Are Smarter than the Few,* London: Little, Brown.

Tuckman, Bruce W. (1965) "Developmental sequence in small groups," *Psychological Bulletin,* 63, pp. 384–99.

Index